TOUGH TARGET

Detective J. J. Bittenbinder
with William Neal

RUNNING PRESS
PHILADELPHIA · LONDON

Library of Congress Cataloging-in-Publication Number 96-070631

ISBN 0-7624-0090-0

Cover photograph © 1997 by Jim Graham
Cover designed by Ken Newbaker
Edited by Tara Ann McFadden

This book may be ordered by mail from the publisher. Please include $2.50
for postage and handling. *But try your bookstore first!*

Running Press Book Publishers
125 South Twenty-second Street
Philadelphia, Pennsylvania 19103-4399

DEDICATION

To conduct a homicide investigation, you start at the body on the scene and work backwards to find the motive, the circumstances, and the killer. If you go back one step further, you learn how the killer picked his victim. This book is dedicated to the victims of violent crime during whose investigations I learned this process. I will continue to dedicate my life to teaching others how to keep themselves safe.

From everyone connected with this book and all the people who will benefit from reading it, I thank the silenced souls.

ACKNOWLEDGMENTS

Special thanks to: Associated Locksmiths of America, National Association of Bunko Investigators, National Coalition Against Domestic Violence, Patricia Lofthouse, Richard Paskin, Tim Powers, Safe Campuses Now, and Security on Campus, Inc.

I wish to gratefully acknowledge the help and support I received from my entire family, my police partners during my career with the Chicago Police Department, the J. Marc Group, and Speakers International.

CONTENTS

FOREWORD

I first saw J. J. Bittenbinder on a hot August night in 1989. A series of vicious crimes had paralyzed Chicago's Lincoln Park neighborhoods. A town hall meeting to address the crime wave attracted an overflow audience.

The room had no air conditioning and the heat and humidity were oppressive. The conditions were made worse by the temperament of the audience—people were tense and angry. They wanted answers. What were the police doing to catch these ruthless criminals?

The meeting started at 7 P.M. By nine-thirty, several speakers had come and gone. Some were effective, some were not. As the audience became restless, Commander William Callaghan assured everyone the last speaker would not be easily forgotten. He was right.

Out from the wings emerged a giant of a man with a huge walrus-like mustache, wearing a three-piece suit, a watch fob, and flashy gold rings. His manner was flamboyant and compelling. He began with these words: "My name is J. J. Bittenbinder, and I'm a policeman. . . ."

For the next hour he talked, paced, and performed. I listened and took notes, but most of all I watched the faces in the crowd. As a television producer, I asked myself the question, Are these people ready to change the channel? The answer was obvious. They were captivated by J. J. He was teaching them to be alert and aware; telling them personal safety tips that would help them to overcome their fears and protect their well-being. It was obvious that this man and his message should be shared with millions of others who were hungry for this kind of advice.

I called him the next day. Later that week my business partner, Rick Paskin, and I met J. J. for lunch. We all hit it off well and agreed to bring J. J.'s message to a TV audience. In 1992, in a cooperative effort with KERA-TV and Video Publishing House, a one-hour PBS special was produced that launched J. J. into the national spotlight. A second national PBS special followed later that year.

From that time it's been a remarkable journey. J. J. now delivers his presentations all over the world. He has been featured in countless stories in popular magazines and regularly appears as a guest on national television programs. *Good Morning America* tapped into him as their crime expert and he hosted his own national weekly television series, called *Tough Target*. J. J. continues to deliver his message to the masses through ongoing guest appearances and as host of his own television program.

I am involved in writing, producing, and directing most of J. J.'s television work and I'm often asked, "What's he really like?" Well, he's not much different off-camera than on-camera. What you see is what you get—a modern-day mix of Dirty Harry and John Wayne.

My favorite J. J. story is one recounted by his close friend Larry Flood, Chicago police officer and now attorney. Larry's first experience with J. J. is an unforgettable story.

"I was a rookie cop and had heard stories about the man," recalls Flood. "But it didn't prepare me for the real thing. I remember it was a cold, late Saturday night, maybe 2 A.M. We were on patrol and got a call that there was a man with a gun in a bar at Clark Street and Leland Avenue. A tough part of town. A tough bar. The report said he was drunk, armed, and angry.

"We were the first of several squad cars that converged on the scene. As we got out of our cars, the last squad car roared in, jumped the curb, and screeched to a halt at the front door of the bar.

"Two 'Blues' hopped out. J. J. was wearing his leather jacket, collar turned up, with a white scarf around his neck. He had holsters on both hips. He said nothing, but quickly moved to the entrance of the bar, where he dashed through the front door with a gun in each hand. His partner, Bobby, was right behind him and we were right behind Bobby. It was smart to be behind Bobby—he was carrying a shotgun.

"Inside, J. J. saw a waitress he knew, and after giving her a big kiss hello on the cheek, asked her, 'Where's the sonofabitch with the gun?'

"Meanwhile, the guy with the gun—a big biker type—was seated at a booth in the back with a gun resting on his lap. The other cops and I ushered the frightened patrons out the door to safety. Then we positioned ourselves behind the bar, guns at the ready, while J. J. and Bobby made their move. They were quick, aggressive, and smart.

"They pulled the guy out of the booth, grabbed the gun, slammed him to the floor, and slapped the cuffs on him. He didn't know what hit him and it was all over in a few seconds. When the dust settled, I said to my partner, 'So that's J. J. Bittenbinder?' My partner just nodded and smiled."

That's J. J. the cop, with the hard-edge personality common to most big-city detectives. And at six feet four inches tall and 225 pounds, he can be very intimidating. The bad guy's worst nightmare.

That hard edge that you first see melts when he reads the letters from those who have followed his advice and avoided violent crimes such as rape, maybe even murder. Many begin something like this: "Detective Bittenbinder—I want to thank you for saving my life!" Those letters bring tears to his eyes.

John Wayne used to save the day like that. But John Wayne and Dirty Harry did their thing in the movies. In real life, the stakes are higher—it's the real deal! And when you're on the streets, there is no Dirty Harry or John Wayne or even J. J. Bittenbinder at your side. You're out there all alone. And no one recognizes that more than J. J.

That is the reason this book is loaded with hard-hitting advice to keep you safe. It's not fancy or complicated. It's simple and practical. And it could save your life— if you *listen* and *act* on what J. J. tells you.

—**William Neal**

INTRODUCTION

"My name is J. J. Bittenbinder, and I'm a policeman."

For the past fifteen years, I've said those words to groups large and small, old and young, from all walks of life. It's how I open my presentation on being a Tough Target.

I've been a police officer since 1971. I spent most of my career as a homicide detective in Chicago. I've handled double murders, triple murders, robberies, and rapes. I've interviewed more than a thousand victims of violent crime. I've also interviewed the witnesses and offenders.

I've seen a lot of crime, and I've learned a lot. To solve a homicide, the detective works backward from the body to the incident to the circumstances and finally to the identification of the offender. Sharing my experiences as a detective can help keep you from becoming another victim of crime.

In this book I'm the lifeguard and you are one of many swimmers in the shallow waters. And out in the deep water are the sharks. Every once in a while a shark comes into the shallow water and picks off a victim. If we can't keep the sharks away from the swimmers, then we must take the swimmers out of the water. But if we can teach the swimmers how to keep the sharks away themselves, then they can swim in safety. This is true empowerment. I want you to be able to do something for yourself besides calling 911.

The sharks are out there. They really are. If you don't know how to deal with them, you can never go into the water without danger or fear.

If two people are standing on a corner, the tough one never gets picked as a victim. That's not because the bad guys are smart. They might be stronger than you and they might be faster than you, but they are not smarter than you. The bad guys just have excellent instincts for selecting their victims.

When the lion chases the antelope across the plain, the lion never goes after the swiftest or the strongest antelope. The lion doesn't want a challenge, the lion wants a meal. When a bad guy steps out of an alley to select a robbery victim, he doesn't pick the toughest one either. When the burglar walks down the street, he doesn't say, "Look at that house over there—it looks like the toughest one on this whole block. I think I'll try it." No, the burglar selects the easy house. The one with the open door or the broken window or the one without the home security sign on the front lawn.

I was the first detective on the murder scene of a woman who had been shot in the head and stuffed into a garbage dumpster. I've seen how stray bullets from drive-by shootings take the lives of children playing in their own homes. I've seen teenagers mutilated in a drug deal gone bad. I've investigated murder victims who were stabbed, shot, beaten, choked, and killed every other way you can think of. I've held the hand of a murdered child and felt the warmth still coming from his tiny body.

These are things no human being should ever have to see. I want to keep you from seeing what I've seen. I'm going to tell you how the bad guys pick their victims, how not to be selected as a victim, and what to do if you are selected. Plain and simple, I want to make you—and those close to you—Tough Targets.

The best way for me to communicate my message is with the liberal use of stories. True stories involving ordinary people in everyday places, because that's where crime strikes. To explain a point, I will sometimes use stories that involve violence and end in tragedy. That's the nature of my business. It's just the way it is. When I recount these stories it's for one reason and one reason only: I find that if I'm not dramatic and sometimes graphic, the point is missed. And if you miss the point, I haven't done my job.

You also need to understand that there are no absolutes and nothing works every time. This is a book about how not to become a victim. The purpose is to make suggestions that will be in the forefront of your mind *when* you need them. You'll find a lot of stories of success and personal empowerment involving people just like you who have faced a predator and avoided becoming his prey. Maybe it's happened to you or someone close to you.

So here we go. We'll take this journey together. I will give you options. I will teach you how to be in control of your own personal safety. That's empowerment! That's being a Tough Target!

The Beginning of Tough Target

My first presentation was in the summer of 1980. There had been a series of violent rapes on Chicago's north-side lakefront community. The rapist was committing one a night. He was known as a "screen cutter": He gained entry by cutting the screens and going through the windows or doors.

The community was in an uproar. The town officials called a meeting and asked for police detectives familiar with these types of cases to attend. The group numbered about sixty people—mostly women. Some were afraid, and all were concerned. Since police detectives aren't allowed to speak about cases that are under investigation and I didn't know who was in the room, I didn't want to give out any information about the investigation, but I felt the need to help these people.

When it was my turn to talk, I explained that I wasn't able to answer specific questions. I did, however, explain how they could keep the windows open and be safe at the same time. That first time I spoke about twenty minutes. Two months later I was asked to speak at a crime-prevention meeting. Again I spoke for twenty minutes. Then the speeches occurred once a month and lasted forty minutes. Soon it became once a week for an hour. I spoke to parent–teacher groups, grade schools, high schools, colleges, seniors, and other organizations of concerned citizens.

For the next ten years I delivered presentations all over Chicago in schools, community halls, and church basements. By day I'd track down predators. By night I'd keep people from becoming their prey.

Fear of Crime: Fact or Fiction?

Crime is not the number-one issue in America today. The number-one issue is the fear of crime. People are afraid. It doesn't have to be that way. Much of that fear is due to the randomness of so many criminal acts and conflicting reports on the extent of the problem.

In January 1996 a *Time* magazine feature story led with this headline: "Law and Order: Crime rates are down across the U.S.—some dramatically. Is this a blip or a trend? With so many factors in play, it may be a bit of both." Very promising. And yet the Council on Crime in America, a bipartisan private body headed by former U.S. attorney general Griffin Bell and former drug czar William Bennett, paints a very different picture. Their 1996 report declared: "America is a ticking violent crime bomb." It said the crime rate—based on surveys of victims and not just crimes reported to the police—shows the incidence of violent crime was

5.6 times higher in 1993 than what was reported. Based on victims' reports, there were nearly 11 million violent crimes, compared to the roughly 2 million officially reported.

Which information is accurate? I'd like to believe that crime in America is decreasing, but having been a policeman for twenty-five years, I think that the Council on Crime report is probably closer to the truth. The bottom line is this: Nobody really knows. The incidence of reported crime is not an accurate measure because so few crimes are reported. When crime reports and predictions are based on faulty, manipulated, or incomplete data, they cannot be accurate. The available statistics are hollow. For this reason, the statistics in this book cannot be taken as law. Also for this reason, there's a lot of confusion and fear about crime out there. **Crime can happen to anyone, anytime, anywhere. It can happen to you.**

The Four Laws of the Jungle

To protect yourself and your family, you need to understand that there are four laws of the jungle.

The First Law

Crime can happen to anyone, anytime, anywhere. It can happen to you. It's the faulty-logic equation. The bad guy says, "I won't get caught," and the victim says, "It won't happen to me." They're both wrong.

You may live in a nice neighborhood, shop at nice malls, send your kids to nice schools; because you do these things you think you're safe. When a man wants to hunt deer, he goes where the deer are. When the criminal wants to steal or rob, he goes where the better targets are.

Which group do you think would be less likely to lock their doors: the poor, the middle class, or the wealthy? Of course it's the wealthy. They reside in locations where they believe it won't happen to them, and it may not. On the other hand, how much trouble is it to lock the doors? It is always better to protect what you have than to complain when it is gone.

Don't think it's just the other guy's problem. It may become your problem too!

The Second Law

Bad guys don't all look like Charles Manson, Freddie Krueger, or Bluto. The bad guys look like fathers and uncles and neighbors because they *are* fathers and uncles and neighbors.

It's easier to believe bad things about people we don't know than to believe someone we know is evil. John Wayne Gacy dressed up in a clown suit and attended parties for the children in the neighborhood. He later became known as "The Killer Clown" for murdering thirty-three young boys and burying their bodies under his house. Ted Bundy had movie-star looks, which he used to lure women into his car. It was a one-way trip for forty-five of those women. Jeffrey Dahmer, who cannibalized some of his young victims, looked like a normal guy. My point is this: You cannot pick out a serial killer on the street by the way he walks or the color of his hair.

The Third Law

It's not how tough you are, it's how tough the bad guy thinks you are. It's all in your attitude and body language. Always walk and carry yourself in a confident manner. Keep your head up. Predators are always looking up at other things. The prey look at the ground. So if you don't want to be prey, look like a predator. He doesn't know you or anyone else walking down the street. So how does he select his victim? He picks the weak-looking one—and that can't be you. There are three things that the bad guy does not want to have happen:

• he doesn't want to be physically defeated by his victim

• he doesn't want to be identified

• he doesn't want to be caught by the police

The only one that bad guy has control over is the first one. He picks people he perceives to be the easy victim. He identifies the targets by the way they look. If you look tough you won't be selected as a victim. You don't need to scowl at everyone you see, but when you walk down the street keep your head up and let your eyes sweep over the faces of the people walking toward you. If you stand on any corner and watch people walking, you'll observe that when a man and woman walk toward one another they will get to a certain distance and the woman will look away. She looks away because she thinks that if she doesn't she'll encourage a remark she doesn't want to hear. So she looks away—mistake! There is a way to look away and not look like a victim. When you shift your eyes, look to the left or to the right. Just don't look down. Lowering your head or eyes is the body language trademark for subservience. If you look vulnerable and weak, you will be selected.

In sports, players are taught to find the other team's weakness and capitalize on that in order to persevere. The bad guy also will look for a weak spot or a chink in the armor of society. He will then strike and take what he wants.

I've been throwing bad guys up against the wall for years and I've never yet found a Mensa card in any of their pockets. We're not dealing with rocket scientists, but the bad guys have excellent instincts and they look for vulnerable targets. If you're tougher than the next person, or if the bad guy thinks you are, you won't get picked. And you won't be a victim. That's just the way it is.

It's not how tough you are. It's how tough he thinks you are.

The Fourth Law

You are responsible for yourself. You've got to be prepared because the bad guy is prepared. When this guy steps into the arena he knows what he's going to say, what he's going to do, what he's going to take, and where he's going to run. What does the victim know? Nothing. That's why the bad guys win—every time!

As with any two competitors—armies, corporations, individuals, or football teams—when one is prepared and one isn't, you know who is going to win.

FOUR-PART TOUGH TARGET STRATEGY

There are four laws of the jungle, and four parts to your Tough Target strategy.

Part One

Have a plan and keep it simple. You need to know before you step into the arena what your options are and how you will react to a dangerous situation.

Once the crime occurs, it's too late.

The one phrase that is repeated after a crime occurs more than any other: "Officer, it happened so fast!" It is usually followed by: "I didn't get a good look at him, it happened so fast." Or, "I couldn't stop him, it happened so fast." It is repeated so often that police officers don't bother to write it down anymore. Everybody says it.

It happens too fast to figure it out "on the fly." It's not like on television and in the movies, where the crime goes down in slow motion. You see the victim, cut to the offender, cut back to the victim, cut back to the offender. In the meantime the camera is performing a slow dance to the sound of the music. That's not how it happens in real life. It happens BOOM in real time, which gives you virtually no time to figure out what to do.

A purse snatch takes two seconds; some of the confrontational robberies take ten seconds. If you are averaging four to six seconds and he's ready and you're not, you know who is going to win. You need to have a plan.

You need to know what you're going to do. This is based on your abilities and your strengths. A complicated plan has too many decisions in it. You will not have the time to make those decisions. Have a plan and keep it simple.

Part Two

Deny privacy. Don't get in the car! Remembering this rule can save your life. What do you do if you're approached by some guy with a weapon and he says, "Get in the car and you won't get hurt!" Do you believe him? Do you go with him? After all, he has a weapon. What if it's your child? The answer is No! No! No! Never go with the offender. Deny him the opportunity to get you to a private place.

Part Three

Attract attention. What can you do to scare off an attacker? Yell "Fire! Fire! Fire!" at the top of your lungs and run like hell. Don't be embarrassed—this is your life we're talking about. Others will hear your cries and come to your rescue.

Part Four

Take action. Do something to this guy. No matter how well prepared you are, there are times when the bad guy will be in your face and you have no other choice but to fight back. And if fleeing is an option, it is always your best option.

Every morning in Africa, a gazelle wakes up. It knows it must run faster than the fastest lion or it will be killed. Every morning a lion wakes up. It knows that it must outrun the slowest gazelle, or it will starve to death.

So, it doesn't matter whether you are a lion or a gazelle: When the sun comes up you'd better be ready.

BOOK I

Chapter 1

HAVING A PLAN

The first part of your Tough Target strategy is to have a plan. You need to know ahead of time what you are going to do if you're in a compromising situation.

Think Like the Bad Guys Think

Now goofs is a term I use a lot to describe bad guys. You'll see it throughout this book. Someone asked me once why I call them goofs. My answer: Because that's what they are. So . . . goofs it is. There are a lot of goofs out there, but one thing they know how to do is keep it simple. They pick their victims on a vulnerability scale. The most vulnerable one is the one who gets it. It's all about targets of opportunity. The bad guy doesn't leave his house in the morning and say, "I'm gonna steal cars today," or "I'm just gonna steal wallets today," or "I'm just gonna do smash-and-grabs today." If he sees an opportunity to steal a car, that's what he takes. Or if he sees an easy purse snatch, he'll go for the purse—targets of opportunity.

I compare these goofs to sharks. A shark is the most effective killing machine on this planet. But even a shark does not come by at thirty-five miles an hour and snap somebody's head off. That's not the way it happens. What does the shark do? The shark bumps its prey and then comes back around to take it. He does this because he has bad eyesight but has sensors on his head to help identify the prey.

That's just the way the goofs on the street do it, but the bump can be verbal. He'll come up to you and ask a question. He wants to see the fear in your eyes. He wants to hear the fear in your voice when you answer his questions. Sometimes he'll get right in your face and say, "Hey, you got a cigarette?" "Which way is Clark Street?" "You got change for a dollar?" This guy is invading your space. And when he asks for change, there's always one victim out there who's going to grab for his wallet and say, "No, all I got is this twenty!" Is this guy vulnerable? Of course.

What should you do when someone shady-looking approaches? Yell "No!" and get out of there. No hesitation. It's "No!" and get your knees in the breeze. Remember, if fleeing is an option, it is always your best option.

It doesn't matter if this guy is legit or not. Maybe he really did just want to know where Clark Street is and he's left standing there looking like a fool. And maybe you're a little embarrassed. That's okay too. You'll get over it and so will he. You're safe and that's what counts. Because there's no way for you to know who's legit and who isn't, and you shouldn't be guessing. Not on the street.

Three Women

Having a plan also means being smart in going about your everyday business. Let's take purses, for example. The goofs go for purses because women tend to keep everything in their purse: cash, credit cards, keys, everything. Men usually spread their things around. They have keys in one pocket, their wallet with credit cards in another, and a money clip with cash somewhere else. If the guy grabs a woman's purse, he gets everything: money wallet, credit cards, even house keys. Women are often perceived as physically easier targets as well.

Consider three women walking down the street. The first woman I'll call Barbara. Busy Barbara. She's got her purse over her shoulder. She is carrying her trenchcoat over one arm, her briefcase, and her umbrella, and she's talking on her cell phone. Where's her purse? The strap is over her right shoulder, and the purse is bouncing off her right hip as she walks down the street. It almost floats out there. That's woman number one.

Woman number two is a little tougher—Tess. Now Tess carries her purse with the strap across her body. If there's a flap on the purse, it's toward her. And when she walks down the street, she's got a grip on this purse. Man, she's got that baby!

Let's move on to woman number three. She is real tough. Real Tough Rita. Rita keeps her purse just like Tess—with the strap across her body—only Rita puts her purse on first and then puts on her coat.

Barbara, Tess, and Rita were walking down the street, one behind the other. And some thug comes out of the alley to steal a purse. Whose purse is he going to take? Barbara's, of course. Every time! Not because she's younger or older or weaker or stronger but because she's more vulnerable. She doesn't look prepared and she's preoccupied with talking on the phone.

There's an even better option than putting your purse under your coat, and that's a fanny pack. Fanny packs are compact and easily concealed beneath a coat, a jacket, or even a sweater. I like them because the goofs don't! And not only are they tough to see, they are even tougher to pull off someone's body. I highly recommend fanny packs for anyone, but I especially encourage older people to carry one. If you put an older woman in that group with Tess and Rita and Barbara—and that senior woman is wearing a fanny pack under her sweater where the bad guys can't see it—which of these women will become the victim? You got it. It's still Barbara!

Awareness

If you were walking along a path in the jungle and you heard a twig snap behind you, would you turn around? Of course you would. But you're in the city or on a suburban street and you hear a car door slam, or you hear the sound of running feet. What do you do? Many people don't turn around and look. Many just keep looking at the ground and say, "Gee, I hope he runs by me." You can't do that. You've got to turn around. You've got to check it out. Is it two guys playing ball? Is it some kid running after his sister? Or is it some lunatic chasing a little old lady with an ax?

Whatever it is, you've got to be aware of your surroundings at all times. You need time to react. That's being prepared. That's having a plan. And if you think you are being followed, cross the street and get to a place where there are people. When you do, tell somebody! Call the police! Remember, if you aren't the victim, someone will be. The bad guy is going to hit someone. He will select, approach, and strike at the one he perceives to be the most vulnerable. If he thinks you are prepared, because you look prepared and look tough, you won't be picked.

What do you do if you are approached? Do you acknowledge a stranger? Here's what often happens when a woman is approached. There comes a point when the woman gets uncomfortable and looks away. She may feel that if she doesn't look away, she may be encouraging a comment from this guy. So she looks away, most often down.

She's saying "I'm weak" or "I don't want to be here." Instead, meet that person's gaze for just a moment, so he knows you are aware of him. And then look straight ahead. If someone stops in a car and says, "Do you know . . . ?" "Have you got . . . ?" "Can you spare . . . ?" Just say, "No!" Don't engage in a conversation. Trust your instincts and get out of there.

- Have a plan and be committed to it.
- Keep your plan simple.
- Look like a predator, not like the prey.

- If you think you're being followed, go where there are people.
- Beware of the bump.
- If fleeing is your best option, get your knees in the breeze.

Sonia Choquette

There's a very talented woman in Chicago by the name of Sonia Choquette. She's a psychic. Like most people, I'm skeptical of psychics, but some of Sonia's results are impressive. She has become a celebrity in Chicago and has gained a national reputation as a successful writer and teacher.

One of Sonia's fundamental principles is awareness. It's the key to developing psychic abilities, which Sonia teaches are within each of us. When it comes to personal safety, the awareness factor is critical.

According to Sonia, an act of aggression, just before it happens, evokes a change in energy that can be sensed and felt if you are aware of your surroundings. Those moments, even split seconds, before a crime happens can mean the difference between life and death. Call it instinct or an energy force, it's the same thing. Be aware of your surroundings and trust your instincts.

Trust your instincts. When the hair on the back of your neck stands up, that's millions of years of evolution telling you to get out of there.

The Confrontation

In a robbery confrontation, each participant will tell the other the things that are the most important to that person at the time. In the first verbal exchanges, the bad guy will usually say, "Be quiet! Give me your money! Don't look at me! Hurry!"

The victim will say, "Don't hurt me."

So let's look at a situation that is more than just some guy who grabs a purse and runs. There's a bad guy with a gun, and he spots a woman leaving the office late at night. Suddenly this guy is waving his pistol in her face, pushing her into an alley, and demanding money. She unzips her purse and gives him all of her money.

WOMAN: Don't hurt me, here's the money.

HE TAKES THE MONEY.

BAD GUY: Now I want that ring, hurry up.

WOMAN: It was my grandmother's.

BAD GUY: I don't care. I won't hurt you, just give me the ring.

HE TAKES THE RING. NEXT COMES THE WATCH, THE BRACELET, THE PEARL NECKLACE, THE CREDIT CARDS.

Be quiet, pull down those pants.

WOMAN: But you said you weren't going to hurt me!

HE GRABS HER BY THE ARM AND FORCES HER TO ACT.

BAD GUY: Lady, I don't care about that. I know if you've got your pants around your ankles, you're not gonna chase me outta this alley. Now pull 'em down so I can run away.

SO SHE PULLS DOWN HER SLACKS AND HE RAPES HER.

MAYBE HE EVEN KILLS HER.

You can stop that story anywhere along the line and learn the same lesson. He's lying to her, but he's telling her a lie she wants to believe. And when you tell somebody a lie that they desperately want to believe, they're going to believe it, regardless of how silly it sounds the next day. This woman wanted to believe this guy so badly she did whatever he said. But you can't believe him, because this guy is going to lie and threaten you. He is going to make promises. He will say whatever it takes to get you to do what he wants as fast as he can get you to do it.

You can count on at least one thing from the bad guys: They will always lie!

So what do you do? You give him the money and get out of there. Do not wait around for request number two. The less time you spend with this guy—in front of that weapon—the better it is for you. There is nothing that a woman can carry in her purse, or wear, no piece of jewelry, no designer coat, that is worth risking your life over. None!

The first part of your Tough Target strategy is the simplest part of the whole deal. Everyone can have a plan. You don't have to be big or tough or fast or strong. But you do need to embrace the first law of the jungle. And if you do—if you understand that you can be a victim of crime—then you're on your way. You need to be committed to your plan. Remember, when the goof steps into the arena he knows exactly what he's going to do. And what does the victim know? Nothing. The goof has a plan. The victim doesn't—it's that simple.

Your plan doesn't need to be sophisticated. The simpler the better will work. Martha Reynolds, a sixty-two-year-old woman, had a plan.

MARTHA REYNOLDS

Martha Reynolds had a big day ahead of her. She was up at the crack of dawn and ready to go. She had a doctor's appointment and had to go shopping. Since she didn't own a car, she took public transportation wherever she went.

Martha left the house early in the morning and was the only person at the bus stop. She waited for the bus with her purse hanging over her shoulder. No one else had shown up. Then she noticed this guy coming out of the woodwork and toward her. He was a big, burly guy in his twenties with his chest bursting out of his shirt. Martha watched him and kept stepping closer to the curb. He kept getting closer and closer to her and looking all around. Suddenly he stepped out into the middle of the intersection and looked in all four directions.

Martha knew this guy was not looking for the bus; he was looking to see if there was a cop car nearby. He stepped out into the street, looking in all directions. There were no police cars in sight. So he made his move. He got closer and closer and as he got ready to make his final approach, Martha looked up at him—she looked him straight in the eyes—and said, "Say, don't I know your mother?"

He stopped in his tracks because he wasn't sure! So he didn't do anything except to get outta there—real fast.

Now that's about as basic as you can get. The plan only has to work once. It worked for Martha. She had something to say and something to do. She was prepared. I can't stress it enough, *you need to have a plan.* There just aren't enough police out there for each of us to have one.

You've got to assume that responsibility yourself. The police usually arrive at the scene to take the report after the crime has taken place.

DEANNA TREJO

Twelve-year-old Deanna attended a presentation I gave at her junior high school. I give a lot of talks to young people and it's very gratifying, especially when I heard what happened to Deanna the very next morning. This is the letter I received from Deanna's mother, Candace, a short time later.

Dear Detective Bittenbinder:

I am writing to thank you for saving the life of my twelve-year-old daughter, Deanna. On Thursday, January 12, 1995, at 7:45 A.M., Deanna was three-quarters of a block from school when some guy came up behind her,

grabbed her neck, and said, "Don't turn around, don't look at me, shut up, and don't say anything."

Knowing that the guy was dangerous, my daughter screamed as loud as she could. Our school secretary was on her way to school and she saw the whole incident. She was not sure anything was wrong until she heard the loud scream. At this point the guy took the grip off of my daughter and she ran toward the school secretary who was then coming to rescue her.

When I got the call moments later, I rushed to school. Over and over I thought of what could have happened to her. Just the thought made me ill.

I kept thinking that this was the first time ever that I allowed my seventh-grader to go to school by herself, and it could have been her last. Our family would never have been the same.

I, my husband, and my six children want to thank you for the knowledge that you have given and shared with our family. If not for your Tough Target awareness talk at our school, my daughter would not have known what to do.

When I first talked to Deanna, shortly after the incident, she said to me, "Mom, I'm okay. It was scary but I did everything that J. J. told me to." When she said this to me it made me realize all that you've done. I can never thank you enough for preserving the innocence of my child and possibly saving her life. . . .

CURTESCINE LLOYD

There is no one I know who took having a plan to heart like Curtescine Lloyd. And of all the success stories I tell, this is one I guarantee you will not soon forget. Curtescine lives in Edwards, Mississippi. It's the kind of sleepy Southern town that inspires poets and songwriters, an old-fashioned place where time stands still. But even in a seemingly tranquil setting like this, there are bad guys lurking about. Curtescine came face to face with one of them. Here's how she describes her ordeal:

"I was lying in bed asleep when I was awakened by a noise. I remember looking at the clock, and it was about three A.M. When I looked up, there was this man standing in my bedroom doorway.

"I was scared half to death. I said, 'Please don't kill me. Please don't kill me. I have the keys to my new car on the ironing board and sixty-seven dollars in my purse. Just take it and go, but please don't kill me.'

"He said, 'Oh, I'm gonna take all that after I get what I came for. Shut up, bitch.' He then proceeded to take off all his clothes. And then he slid into bed next to me and pulled my gown up and said he wanted me to perform oral sex on him. Well, I had long ago decided what I would do if anything like this happened. I had a plan. I said, 'All right, come on. Come on. Where is it?'

"Well, at this point he sat in a sitting position on the side of the bed and when he said, 'Here it is!' I grabbed it. I grabbed his penis and I yanked it and I twisted it. Of course he wasn't happy about that so he hit me with a hard blow to the side of the head. Well, I figured I hadn't done enough so I grabbed his scrotum with the other hand and twisted in the opposite direction as if I was wringing out a towel.

He said, 'You're killing me. You're killing me.' And I said, 'Well, you S.O.B., you just won't die for me.' And I got angrier and angrier. So I dragged him down the hallway and out into the living room. He saw the telephone and said, 'Lady, please call the police. Call the police.' I said there was no way I was calling the police. I had a double lock on the door and he was going to open it. So I dragged him to the front door and made him undo both latches. Well, he fell down a couple of times, and I was still holding on, he was begging me to let go.

"At this point, the door opened and I dragged him out to the end of the porch and said, 'When I let go, I'm going to get my gun and blow your BLANK BLANK brains out.' It was a matter of life and death, and I really thought this man was going to kill me. So I gave him another hard twist and then let go of him. He fell down the steps and struggled to try and run, but he was really hurting and he fell down.

"I went into the house, got my aunt's pistol, and came back to the door and fired two shots at him as he was hobbling away. I missed, but that was okay. He was later captured by the police."

These are the kinds of stories that make all my efforts worthwhile. I give about two hundred presentations each year. More than half of these are to schools and senior citizen groups. The young and the old are the most vulnerable. I'm proud of Deanna and Curtescine because they did the right thing. Simply knowing enough to scream and fight back got them the help they needed. There's nothing complicated about that, but it worked. Plain and simple!

You must understand there are no absolutes and nothing works every time. There is nothing I can say—no magic wand I can wave over you—that will make you safe in every situation. The things you can learn here can save your life. If you act on them. That's been the foundation of my message since I began giving talks.

Chapter 2

DENYING PRIVACY

The second part of your Tough Target strategy can save your life. The term "life-saving advice" is not one I throw around loosely so when I say it, I mean it. This information can save your life! Whatever situation you're facing, you need to distance yourself from the potential attacker as soon as possible.

There is a police term—you've heard it in the movies and on television—called the "secondary crime scene." It means the victim was taken to some place other than the place of the initial confrontation. When we deal with a secondary crime scene, it's never pretty. Too often we're looking at rape or murder. The secondary crime scene is the deadliest piece of ground in the world.

The Secondary Crime Scene

There are many tragedies that are simply unavoidable. When it comes to victims of the secondary crime scene, that's another story. Remember, if he wants your property, whatever it is—a purse, a coat, a wallet, a car—you give it up and you get out of there. But if he wants to take you into that car—don't go! If there is ever a line you draw that you're not going to cross, it's this: Never allow yourself to be forced into a car. It's a one-way trip! If he wants to rob you, he can rob you right there. If he's taking you into that car, he's got something else in mind and you can't go. Don't let him get you to a private place. You must deny privacy at all costs. Keep it public, in the open, where it's possible that someone could come and help you.

If ever there is a line you draw that you're not going to cross, it's this: Never allow yourself to be forced into a car. It's a one-way trip!

TAMMY ZYWICKI

You cannot get into a truck either. That's precisely what the authorities believe happened to Tammy Zywicki.

Tammy loved soccer, James Dean movies, and listening to Tom Petty with her two cats, Zorro and Bob. On a hot August day in 1992, Tammy and her younger brother, Daren, packed the car and left their Marlton, New Jersey, home to travel to Evanston, Illinois, where Daren was a student at Northwestern University.

En route, their car overheated. After adding oil, they continued on without further trouble and arrived safely at Northwestern. After spending the night at her brother's apartment, Tammy continued on her journey. Final destination: Grinnel College in Iowa, where she was a senior.

Heading west through Illinois on I-80, she pulled off to the side of the road, perhaps because of more car trouble. No one knows for sure. Several passersby recalled seeing her white Pontiac on the side of the road. Others mentioned seeing a large truck, with unique diagonal markings on the side, pull up behind Tammy's car. The police believe Tammy may have accepted what she thought was a friendly gesture from a friendly truck driver. Perhaps she was offered a short ride to the next service station?

That was the last time Tammy was seen alive. An intense police investigation, and nationwide media coverage, ultimately ended with no leads. Nine days after the Pontiac was abandoned, Missouri police found Tammy's body five hundred miles from the original site. She had been stabbed seven times and raped. Her killer has never been caught.

- Travel with a companion. Never alone. You are a tougher target in the company of someone else.
- Be sure your car is in good running condition.
- If you are stranded, the most important thing you can have is a cellular phone. Use it to call the police.
- Write "Help! Call Police" on a sign and put it in your back window. Someone will call the police for you.
- If a stranger approaches and you sense trouble, tell that person the police are on the way and you expect them to arrive any minute.
- Carry a container of pepper spray in your glove compartment and don't hesitate to use it if you are threatened.

The Cellular Phone

When it comes to safety, a cellular phone is like a spare tire. You hope you never have to use it, but it's there if you do need it. And if you think a cellular phone is too expensive, or you think it's a "luxury" item, consider this: How much is the safety of you and your family worth?

Close to 40 million Americans own wireless phones in 1996, up from 5 million in 1990, and that number is growing daily. Most people who buy cellular phones say their major reason for the purchase is to enhance personal safety.

Authorities estimate that 20 to 25 percent of all 911 calls received come from cellular phones, and about half those callers—an astounding 25,000 a day—don't know where they are. So just as you would on the street, be aware of your surroundings on the road. Take stock of your location as you travel. Then if you get in trouble you can tell the dispatcher where you are. And if you're calling for someone else, make sure you can identify your location before placing the call. It might be a mile marker, or a street sign.

Location-finding technology is either in place or being tested to deal with this problem. Within five years, plans call for technology that will provide dispatchers with the latitude and longitude of a caller to within a city block.

Finally, you also need to know if there is a different emergency number that needs to be dialed in your area. In many states, emergency calls from cellular phones are routed to the highway patrol. So be sure you know the number in your area and find out the number when you travel.

MARY GRAVES

On a sweltering June day in 1995, Mary Graves returned to her parked car in the garage at Tampa International Airport. Her three-year-old daughter was at her side. Mary and her daughter got in the unlocked vehicle and fastened their seatbelts. Suddenly an armed man emerged from the backseat.

He robbed Mary and then, to give himself time to escape, he said he was going to lock Mary in the trunk of her car. But Mary was smart. Just before he pulled her out of the car, she dialed 911 on her cellular phone and gave it to her daughter.

The armed man forced Mary into the trunk and slammed the lid shut. She was trapped. Her chances for survival were slim in that heat. Fortunately her daughter was left alone. She stayed in the car and told emergency operators what had happened to her mother. She also gave them important clues: She could see airplanes and sky.

The operator called airport police, who searched the parking lot. Operators told the girl to honk the horn, something she was not normally allowed to do. But this time, her mother started screaming, "Honk it, baby, you just keep honking."

And she did. The police quickly located the car and freed Mary.

That's a great story! I don't know Mary Graves but I suspect she places a rather high value on that cellular phone. If you do not have a cellular phone, get one! She also locks her car doors now—always!

ELANE CROSBY

In the small town of McAllister, Oklahoma, Elane never thought serious crime could happen. People in her town still leave their doors unlocked when they leave the house. And if homes are left unlocked, why would anyone lock their car doors?

It was a cool evening when Elane made a quick trip to the grocery store. She parked her van near the front door, picked up her groceries, hopped back in the van, and headed for home. As she turned down a side street near her home, she saw movement in the rearview mirror. She knew she was not alone and she knew she was in trouble.

Suddenly, this guy came over the top of the seat and was right in her face. He wrapped a rope around her hand and stuck a knife to her neck. She said, "What do you want? Where do you want me to drive?" Good move. Because the guy was caught off guard. At this point Elane slammed on the brakes, the van slid off the road and into a ditch, and Elane made her escape. He followed in hot pursuit. They struggled and fought right on the street. Elane was stabbed several times and forced back into the van. This time on the passenger side.

He jumped in the driver's side and Elane thought to herself, This is it. I've got one more chance. At that point, as he gassed the van to get out of the ditch, Elane hit the latch of the door. As it burst open, she dived out of the moving vehicle, landing hard on her back. She lay there in a state of semi-consciousness, unaware of how much blood she had lost. Fortunately, the guy in the van had had enough of this feisty woman. He sped off, leaving her for dead. Twenty minutes later, Elane was spotted and taken to a hospital. Emergency surgery saved her from bleeding to death. The van was abandoned, but the guy was never caught.

Elane is one tough lady and one Tough Target. With a rope and a knife in hand, this guy was nothing but trouble. Elane's actions probably saved her life, and I applaud her efforts. Now she locks her van wherever she goes.

Sometimes, no matter how careful and aware you may be, trouble sneaks up on you. It is these times that your plan will not only be your best friend, but it may just save your life. Margie Ann Kline, of Mineral Wells, Texas, is one survivor who knows all about that.

MARGIE ANN KLINE

Margie was lying on her bed watching television, her dog Muffin curled up by her side. It was around midnight. Although she was absorbed in an old movie, thoughts of a recent ordeal were not far from her mind. That ordeal was kidnapping and rape at the hands of Kenneth Wade Garner. She had identified her attacker and he was behind bars, so Margie thought.

But he was not in jail. At that very moment, he was outside her bedroom window! And the television was just loud enough to give him the cover he needed. He was able to remove the window screen and open the window. Suddenly, he burst into the bedroom and was on top of Margie within seconds—gun in hand.

He forced her out of the house, the dog nipping at his heels. Margie said, "We can't take Muffin." He responded, "Where we're going, you won't need her." He told Margie he was taking her to the Ozark Mountains to hide until the statute of limitations on the rape charge ran out. This guy was no rocket scientist, but he was determined and he was dangerous.

Margie had two thoughts: one, that Garner was out of his mind. And two, that she needed a plan to escape. Garner allowed Margie to put the dog back in the house and then forced her into the car.

They began a cross-country journey. As the miles went by, Garner said very little, Margie even less. She was fighting off a growing fear and doing her best to focus on the plan that was taking shape in her mind.

After several hours had passed, Garner stopped for gas. He threatened to shoot her on the spot if she said a word to anyone. Margie believed he was just crazy enough to follow through on his threat, so she needed to be very careful. She asked to go to the washroom and, although he waited outside the door, she put the first part of her plan in place. She took out her lipstick and wrote on the mirror that she had been abducted, described the car and where they were headed.

Sometime after they left, an attendant was told about Margie's message by another customer and called the police. An APB (All Points Bulletin) was issued, but the odyssey continued. Garner never left her side and his threats became more ominous.

Again they stopped, this time at a Wal-Mart in DeQueen, Arkansas. Garner told Margie that if she tried to escape while they were inside the store, he would kill her and anyone else who got in the way. She was convinced he would do it. So now it wasn't just her life on the line, it was other innocent people as well.

With Tennessee and the Ozarks not far off, she knew she had to do something. As Garner paid for the items, Margie pulled a pen and paper from her purse, quickly scribbled a note, and slipped it to the clerk as they were leaving. The clerk read the note, briefly made eye contact with Margie, then calmly turned and waited on another customer. Margie thought she had ignored it. But she hadn't. Instead, she reported it to her manager, who called the police.

By now, since they had crossed state lines, the FBI was involved in the chase. Together with the police, they tracked the fugitive and his hostage to a nondescript roadside motel. They surrounded the motel and Garner eventually surrendered. Margie was freed. Terrified, but unharmed.

I like this story for several reasons. First, Margie survived and the guy was put behind bars. Second, it illustrates the need to have a plan and be prepared. You never know when or where crime will strike. For Margie, it was sitting in her bedroom watching television with her dog.

Third, every situation is unique, and there are certain crimes that happen so fast, and so unexpectedly, that even if you have a plan you may be taken by surprise. Whatever you decide to do, or not do, is ultimately your call, so you need to weigh your options. In order to do that, you must not panic.

If your plan isn't working, figure something else out. Or if you don't really have a plan, you've got to make one up on the fly like Margie did. I don't always recommend doing it that way, but you've got to deal with the hand you are dealt.

Could Margie have done things differently? Maybe. Garner's threats, as real as they seemed to her at the time, were probably idle threats. A dash for freedom when they left the house, at the gas station, or at the store probably would have worked. That's my advice in these situations. You cannot get into that car! Later in the book, I'll explain why I feel so strongly about this.

But Margie did get in that car and she was a hostage. Her life was on the line and she knew it. Despite her fear, she stayed focused on her plan to escape. She didn't give up when she didn't get immediate results, and she didn't give in.

Margie was abducted right in her own home. She had no way of knowing someone was lurking outside her window. He gave her no warning. Usually there is a warning if you trust your instincts. Just before most crimes occur, the hair on the back of your neck stands up and that's your warning. That's millions of years of evolution grabbing you by the back of the neck and telling you, "There's trouble here."

He's Got a Gun!

Let's say you are approaching your car in a parking lot and—BAM—out of nowhere some goof is in your face. And he's got a gun. And he gives you a line that goes something like this: "Trust me, lady. I'm not going to hurt you. Just do as I say and you'll be fine. Now keep quiet and get in the car."

Well, you already know these guys lie. They always lie and they can be very convincing. But you are not going to fall for that lie. So, what do you do with this guy and his gun? Here's the deal: If you break and run immediately, out of one hundred times, how many times do you think this guy is going to shoot? Well, it's low. But I'll give you half. Fifty times out of one hundred he'll shoot.

So out of that fifty times, how many times do you think he's going to hit you with his little pistol while you're running down the street, yelling "Fire"? Well, that number is very low, but I'll give you half again. Now we're down to twenty-five times out of one hundred. And out of that twenty-five times, how many times will it be a serious or fatal injury? I'll give you half again.

So, now we're down to twelve and a half times out of one hundred that you are in serious trouble. That means eighty-seven and a half times out of one hundred you're okay. Scared out of your wits, but okay. And that's a way for me to help you put it all in perspective. The real number, according to the justice department, is less than 5 percent.

Now 5 percent is clearly better than twelve and a half percent, but in either case you can live with those odds. But if you get into the car, he's holding all the aces and your odds are lousy. Why would he be taking you somewhere else? The odds are in your favor. So you have to understand your options. You've got to deny privacy.

Remember the comment the police hear over and over again from victims? It's worth repeating here: "It happened so fast!" That's what they all say! And these crimes do happen fast. That's why having a plan is so important. You need to know how to react in these situations before the crime goes down. No one knows this better than Merri Dee.

MERRI DEE

Merri was a popular television personality in Chicago. As the host of a local talk show, her star was rising. Then Sam Drew was released from prison. Drew was only twenty-six at the time, but he was already a five-time loser who had become infatuated with Merri Dee. On a bitter-cold night in February with barely a week on the streets, he decided to make Merri his own.

As Merri left the studio with a guest from her show, Drew was suddenly in her face. The parking lot was nearly empty, it was dark, and this guy had a gun. He forced his way into the passenger side of the car, pushing Merri's guest next to her. He waved the gun at their heads and told Merri to drive. She did. From one end of the city to the suburbs and all the way into a forest preserve. The whole time this guy was assuring his hostages that they would not be harmed. Just a little night on the town, he told them.

Next, he instructed Merri to pull over and stop the car. The forest preserve was deserted. As they stepped out into the snow, the television guest suddenly made a break for it.

He ran about twenty-five yards but pulled up short of the tree line when Drew yelled, "Halt, or I'll shoot." At this point, Drew grabbed Merri by the arm, pulled her away from the car and toward her guest. Drew still told them, "Relax, nobody's going to get hurt. I'm just going to tie you up so I can get out of here. Now lay down and be quiet."

Well, Drew was lying, of course. As they lay in the freezing cold, Drew put the gun to the head of Merri's television guest and pulled the trigger. He died instantly. Drew then turned to Merri. He stood so close to her that the front part of his foot was on her left arm. He lowered the gun again and, at point-blank range, fired two thirty-eights into her head. He fled, leaving her for dead. Sometime later, Merri and her guest were discovered by a passing motorist.

She miraculously survived the ordeal and went on to be an outspoken advocate of victim's rights. Today, Merri continues her work in television and as a public speaker.

You've seen it a thousand times on television. If a bad guy pulls a gun on you, you do whatever he says. Right? Wrong! Not if it means going down that alley or into that car.

Once again, this all goes back to your plan and being aware. Merri and her guest were simply enjoying a pleasant conversation as they walked to her car. We've all been in that situation. There's nothing wrong with that. Except that all too often these guys will strike when you least expect it. Strength in numbers? Yes, but these guys can be very unpredictable. So be aware of your surroundings at all times. Especially at night.

If you're going to your car, do it quickly, get inside, and lock the doors immediately. Let's assume that's what happened in Merri's situation. That she and her guest got in the car and locked the doors. Now, what do we have? A guy with a gun demanding that she open the door and let him in. But you don't do that. What do you do? Drive away. Blow your horn. Chances are this guy is not going to shoot. Why? Think about it. You're speeding off down the street and he's standing there all by himself.

If he fires that gun, he's going to attract a lot of attention. That's the last thing this guy wants. And if he does fire? He's got a lousy angle. Believe me. I know. I've had that angle, and it's one tough shot. Check it out sometime. Stand just to the left and rear of the car and then imagine that car moving. At night, it's a tougher shot.

Let's say he does force his way into the car. What then? Well, get out of the car! That's right. Take the keys, toss them one way, and run the other. Risky? Of course it is. Will he shoot? Maybe. But these are decisions you must be prepared to make. And consider his options. Again, he can fire that gun and make a lot of noise. Or he can grab the keys and steal your car.

But that's not what happened in Merri's ordeal. She and her guest went with this guy. So let's play it out. Let's go back into the deserted forest preserve just the way it happened.

Merri's guest makes a run for it. Was that a good idea? Absolutely. Was he being a coward leaving a woman behind? Absolutely not! His mistake was that he stopped in his tracks when he was threatened. You can't do that. Keep going. Get out of there. Don't stop. No matter what. Because when you are at the end of the line as these people were, running is probably your only option for survival.

It is also the best chance for anyone left behind. Man or woman. Why? Because if he goes one way, she can flee the other way. And now this guy has a big dilemma. He can't go both ways at once, so he has to decide which of his intended victims to pursue. And even if he catches up with one, the other is sure to be an eyewitness at his trial! And believe me, these guys do not want to go to the slammer.

Chances are, he'll take the car and the purse and cut his losses. Although each situation is different, the one constant is this: As the confrontation escalates, your options become fewer and fewer. The scales tip in his favor. So whatever action you are going to take, make your move right away, or as soon as you can.

- Be aware of your surroundings. Sometimes where you feel the safest is exactly the place this guy is going to strike.
- When you approach your car, have your keys in hand. Don't be fumbling in your pockets or purse.
- Lock your car doors immediately. Then if someone confronts you, he can't get in the car. And if he's got a gun? Drive away. Get out of there.
- If he does force his way into the car, toss the keys and run.
- If you are taken to a private place, your only option is to run. Do whatever it takes.

So far we've looked at situations and events involving the secondary crime scene. But denying privacy also means managing places that can potentially become private. Taxi cabs and other forms of public transportation are a good example.

Public Transportation

How often have you hopped into the backseat of a cab without any idea if the cabbie and that car were legit? Well, here's what you can do. First, stick with the more established cab companies. Second, check out the driver's picture, which is usually part of the registration or license tag. If the picture doesn't match the driver, get out immediately.

Third, note the registration number and make a subtle comment. Say, "Two, two, one, two, I think I'll play that in the lotto tomorrow!" Or, "Two, two, one, two—hey, that's my old address." Now this driver knows that you know the number and you've been very discreet about it. So he's not going to take you around the block, or give you any other hassle.

Buses and trains can also be trouble, especially at night. Here is one simple precaution that will keep you out of danger: Sit near the front by the driver or in the car with the conductor. Now this probably seems obvious, and it is. But you'd be surprised how many people will aimlessly get on a bus or train with no clue what's going on around them.

Consider this situation: One guy is looking to steal a purse, and there are two women and two train cars. One car is completely empty, the other has only the conductor inside. One woman gets on the car with the conductor, the other hops on board the empty car. Which car do you think the guy will get on?

If you've ever been on a bus during rush hour, you'll recognize this situation: People are standing toe-to-toe and there's lots of jostling about as people move in and out of the bus as it makes its stops. Well, this is exactly the kind of environment the savvy pickpocket looks for. He can get close to people easily and can get his hand in and out of a purse or back pocket, as smooth as silk.

So if you deal with this situation, you've got to be especially careful to keep your purse tight against your body, the flap toward you and buckled. For men, put the wallet in the front pocket. The back pocket or inside suit pocket is easy pickin's.

And what do you do if you see someone being victimized by a pickpocket? It's simple. Most buses have curved roofs, and sound reverberates. So you turn around, look up at the ceiling and say loudly, "Get your hand out of her purse!" And every woman on that bus will grab for her purse. And he'll never know who said it. A crime has been averted and you're safe. Not a bad deal.

• Cabs: Check the driver's picture ID. Comment on the registration number.

• Trains & Buses: Sit by the driver or conductor.

Chapter 3

ATTRACTING ATTENTION

The third part of your Tough Target strategy addresses the goof's number one enemy: noise and commotion. If you are in serious trouble or you see someone else in trouble, any attention is exactly what the goof does not want. If you are attacked in your home, your voice is the tool that will save your life.

Before going any further, let's define "serious trouble." Serious trouble is when you are physically in danger of being beaten, raped, or taken into a car. If he wants your property and you give it to him and he gets his knees in the breeze, that's fine. You're safe and that's what is most important. Don't scream at this goof as he is running and have him turn back and shoot you to keep you quiet. Let him go and then call for help.

Serious trouble is if this guy wants you, not your possessions. In that case, I suggest yelling and screaming and kicking for all you're worth. And yell "FIRE! FIRE! FIRE!" rather than simply yelling "HELP!" Fire gets everyone's attention.

Where's the Fire?

If some guy is kicked back in his Lazy Boy recliner, watching *Monday Night Football* with a cold beer in one hand and a big cigar in the other, he's comfortable. Outside he hears a woman struggling with some goof. This guy is trying to drag her into his car. And she's yelling, "Help, police. Help. Help. Help!" Mr. *Monday Night Football* is sitting in his chair and he hears this and he thinks to himself, This is trouble. But it's not gonna cost me any money. I'm not getting involved. I'm not gonna risk getting hurt. So he doesn't get involved.

Same scenario. The guy is in his chair watching the game, only this time the woman is yelling, "FIRE! FIRE! HELP! FIRE!" It's easy. One word over and over again. On that note, Mr. Monday Night is roused from his chair. He's thinking, Now wait a minute. Fire spreads. This could cost me some money. I could get hurt. So he gets involved. He calls 911 and the police arrive on the scene. So that's what you should do. Yell, FIRE!

Yell FIRE! FIRE! FIRE! not HELP! FIRE gets everyone's attention.

At a presentation, one woman asked me what happens if the fire truck comes? Well, that's good. That's great, in fact! Six guys come piling off a truck and the first guy has an ax in his hand. That works! So yell "FIRE" and you'll get some help. Every time.

DAVA GUERIN

It was just before seven A.M. Dava was getting ready for work and was just about to get into the shower when she heard noises coming from another room. She stepped out of the bathroom and there, standing in the middle of her bedroom, was a big hulk of a man wearing a ski mask and gloves.

Without hesitation, he was in her face. But Dava was not about to become a victim. She started screaming, "FIRE! FIRE! FIRE!" at the top of her lungs while she fought this guy off as best she could. After a short, frantic struggle he punched her in the face, knocking her off her feet.

He then jumped on top of her and the battle continued right on the floor. He tried to cover her mouth but she resisted; her screams now became even louder. They fought for what seemed like an eternity to Dava but was really only a couple of minutes.

Then with one desperate kick she was able to break loose of her attacker and run downstairs to the front door. Meanwhile, this goof was in hot pursuit and really on a mission of destruction. Dava, fortunately, had the presence of mind to get the door unlocked and once she managed that, she ran to a neighbor's condo. Within three minutes, the police—and, yes, the fire department too—arrived on the scene.

Dava credits her escape to one thing. "My voice is what saved me. My burglar alarm did not work, nothing was there to help me but my voice. And it was yelling Fire that did it. Yelling Help probably would not have got anyone involved because people are afraid. So if I didn't know to yell Fire, there's no telling what would have happened to me. I could have been raped, murdered, who knows what."

Dava is right, of course. At the very least, this guy had rape on his agenda. But thanks to her quick thinking, Dava escaped with a few bruises and a black eye. Some say she was lucky. I say she was tough and smart. There's a difference. It's called making your own luck.

Other Types of Noise

Keep in mind that there are a lot of ways to attract attention. A car alarm, for example. You are walking down the street and half a block away you hear it: BEEP! BEEP! BEEP! HONK! HONK! You don't think much of it, other than that these things can be quite annoying. But put yourself in the shoes of the goof. He's trying to break into this vehicle by being as quiet as a church mouse. Then the alarm goes off and suddenly his little world erupts into a carnival. Even though you and everyone else around there ignore the alarm, he's the one guy who can't. So he's going to move on and go for a car that's not such a Tough Target. That's what these guys do.

It's the same thing if you are attacked and you start screaming FIRE! It doesn't matter if there's anybody around there to hear you or not. But it does matter to the goof because he can't take that chance. He'll react like there is someone who will hear you, and that hesitation can be what you're looking for to make your break.

You've got to play it like you're alone out there. You've got to play it like there are no police. The police can't be everywhere, especially when these crimes happen. They come later to take the report.

You've got to play it like you're alone out there.

You've got to play it like there are no police.

Help Others

The cellular phone can save your life, and you can use it to help someone else. Let's say you're driving down the street and some guy is being mugged.

You don't know if the bad guy has a gun or knife but you know that someone is in serious trouble. You can't ignore it but you also don't want to put yourself in danger. Keep your distance, roll down your window *halfway*, and yell, "Get away from her. I'm calling the police!" It doesn't matter if you have a cellular phone or not, but it does matter to this goof. He can't take that chance. At the very least, you've created a distraction and the opportunity for the victim to make a break. If he starts moving toward your car, wait until he gets about halfway there, then drive away. This gives the woman time to escape.

Do You Need a Gun?

What about a real weapon? What if Dava had a gun hidden in her bedroom? Let's say it was in the drawer of her nightstand. Well, this is pure speculation, of course, but let's play it out. Let's assume when this goof came into her house, Dava went for the gun instead of using a natural weapon—her voice. Let's assume, under this hypothetical situation, she was able to break away and had a moment to pull the gun from the drawer. And then she faced off with this guy. She's holding the gun and he moves toward her.

In my experience, here's the way it usually comes down. The person holding the gun will hesitate. Why? Because she knows that what she is about to do is a final act that cannot be changed, undone, erased, or altered in any way. That is spinning around in her head. Then there's a moral issue. And there's the fear of being sued. It all comes down to one question: Am I sure? So she hesitates. And the more intelligent she is, the longer the hesitation. But the bad guy doesn't hesitate. He'll grab the gun and pop her with it. Because he doesn't care about being sure.

Try this one out yourself. When you talk to your friends set up this scenario: You're standing there with a gun in your purse and some guy comes up to rob you— would you pull the gun out and kill him? The length of the time from the end of your question to the time of their response is how long it would take to talk themselves into saying yes. And for that person to actually take action is going to take two or three times that.

Guns in the hands of citizens don't work because people hesitate in using them! If they did work, the police would have an easy job. The police would come out on the streets every morning and scoop up dead bad guys. But that's not how it is. The police come out on the streets every morning and find dead good guys, women, and children.

CYNTHIA GRIMSON

Cynthia, a Nashville record executive, was leaving her office on Music Row in broad daylight. As she opened the front door of her car, she was grabbed from behind and ordered into the vehicle.

But Cynthia was tough and refused to be a victim. Instead of getting into the car, she screamed at the top of her lungs. The bad guy took a few steps back from her and said, "Stop screaming. Stop screaming." She never even considered letting the guy get her into a car. Meanwhile, several co-workers inside the building heard Cynthia's screams, ran outside, and caught a glimpse of the attacker, who was fleeing the scene in high gear. Loud screaming is every bad guy's nightmare!

One of Cynthia's co-workers jumped in his car and followed the man, and called the police on his cellular phone. The police apprehended the attacker and he went to jail.

This is another story that really makes me proud. It is also a great way to illustrate the fact that it's not only about attracting attention but also about denying privacy and helping one another out.

How to Fight Back

- If you are attacked and choose to fight back, give it everything you've got.
- If you are knocked down, swivel around on your backside and kick for all you're worth.
- Go for the groin, shins, eyes, or throat. These are his most vulnerable areas.
- Yell FIRE! FIRE! FIRE! Fire gets everyone's attention.
- If you see or hear someone else in trouble, do something.

Chapter 4

TAKING ACTION

Everyone wants money, right? The bad guys are no exception. And they always have a plan to get your money. The fourth part of your Tough Target strategy is to take action. Here's how you can take action and keep your hard-earned money.

The Two-Second Hit

Some crimes are referred to as the two-second hit. These crimes come down fast. Let's use purse snatching as an example. If someone goes for your purse—and you don't have a plan—you are betting that you can formulate one and react in two seconds or less. That's how long it takes to snatch a purse.

Some guy comes out of nowhere, from behind, maybe he scares you half to death, and you've got to prepare in less than two seconds. Is that realistic? No! So you've got to know what you're going to do before the crime comes down.

If fleeing is an option, it is always your best option.

L et's look at the two-second hit again, only this time our victim is using three out of the four parts of the Tough Target strategy. She had a plan so she is carrying a money clip in the outside pocket of her purse. The money clip holds a five-dollar bill wrapped around two singles. When the guy appears and demands money, but she thinks he wants a lot more than just her money.

What does she do? She reaches inside that purse, pulls out the money clip, shows him the money, and says, "This is all I got!" And then what happens? She flings the money clip one way and she runs in the opposite direction. There's no hesitation. The money goes one way and she goes the other. And she's yelling, "Fire! Fire! Fire!"

So what have we got here? The guy is standing there wondering what just went wrong with his little robbery scheme. This woman—a bundle of noise—is running away screaming "Fire!" And the money is sitting over there on the sidewalk all by itself, nice and quiet. Where do you think this guy is going to go? Well, I can tell you, most of the time he's going for the money; and then he's going to run away.

Why a money clip? Why not just toss the money? Well, it's simple. If you toss money, it floats. If you toss a money clip, it has weight and it carries. You want that money as far away from him as you can get it. Buy a cheap money clip. A shiny metal one is the best. The metal will allow you to throw it farther and it will be easier for him to see it in low-light situations at night.

Here's something else I want you to remember. It is an excellent idea for a woman to keep her keys out of her purse. It gives her more options. Let's say a woman is walking out of a shopping mall, into the parking lot to her car. From behind her a silent figure runs up and snatches her purse off of her shoulder. It's gone. He jumps into a waiting car and drives off. She screams and runs back into the mall to call her husband. She tells him what happened and he says, "Stay in the mall and wait for me, I'll get a baby-sitter." The baby-sitter comes over to stay with the kids and the husband races to the mall. Well, this husband has a two-way trip. The bad guys only have a one-way trip. They can be at the house with the baby-sitter, the kids, the TV, and the stereo before these folks can get back. They have the keys and the address from her driver's license. If not tonight, maybe tomorrow.

Maybe this woman is smarter than that. When she calls her husband and he says he's on his way, she tells him to stay put. She says, "You stay home, I'll take a cab. But stand out in front and pay for it, I don't have any money." Now, the bad guys see her get into a cab and they can go back and steal the car. They have the keys! Or maybe they'll do it the next night or a week later.

Now, let's change it again. The same woman, the same parking lot, the same guy, but this time the keys are not in her purse. He snatches the purse and runs away. She still screams, but she no longer has to ask assistance of anyone. She just gets into the car and drives home. She doesn't have to wait in the lot for her husband. The bad guys might have the address from her license, but since they don't have the keys, they can't get in. She doesn't even have to have the locks changed on the car or the house.

I usually tell women to keep their keys in a pocket instead of their purse. If you have no pocket, buy a waistband key holder from a hardware store or locksmith. Put the keys on it and hang it inside your skirt or pants.

You do not have to spend a lot of money to be safe. You just have to think ahead and have a plan. Another popular place the bad guys tend to target is banks; remember—that's where the money is. Marla Sacks can attest to that.

MARLA SACKS

Marla left her office to run some errands and stopped at the bank in a strip mall. It was about one-thirty in the afternoon. She never thought there could be any kind of trouble so she never worried about it or took precautions.

She needed to withdraw a large sum of cash from her savings account. So she went to the counter and filled out a savings withdrawal slip. What she didn't know was that she was being watched. She was handed her cash, put it in her purse, and left the bank.

Marla got in her car and a few blocks later felt the steering wheel pull to one side. She suspected it was a flat tire so she pulled over to the side of the road and checked it out. She was now in an area of unfamiliar territory with a flat tire. A car pulled over and a well-dressed man offered to help fix the tire. Marla still didn't sense any danger, until he pulled the gun out. She was shocked. He ordered her to sit on the ground, grabbed her car keys and purse, got back in his car, and drove off down the street. In less than a minute, her life had been endangered and she lost more than $2,000. She was so shaken up she didn't think to get the number of his license plate until he was too far away for her to read it.

The license plate number may have helped, but chances are the car was stolen anyway. What happened here?

The guy hanging around outside the bank scopes out those coming in. Marla looked well-to-do and trusting of her environment. Each bank color-codes its deposit and withdrawal slips. The colors indicate to the teller, at a glance, what the customer wants to do. The bad guy knew too. He knew what color the savings withdrawal slips are and he knew the savings withdrawal slip probably means big bucks. So, he watches her pick up that slip and fill it out. At some banks you can even see from outside the bank or in the lobby.

He also notes which car she was driving. Then as Marla moves into the teller line, this guy walks over to her car, pulls out an ice pick, and stabs once through the tire. In about three blocks the tire will be flat. That's three blocks away from the bank and the security guards and the cameras. You know the rest of the story. And even though Marla lost a lot of money, she was still lucky because this guy could have taken the cash *and* Marla.

What can we do to protect ourselves in this situation? We can't force the banks to change the color of their withdrawal slips, but you can go to the bank counter, away from others, to select and fill out the slip. Or take some of each of the slips with you and fill them out in the privacy of your own home. That's a good plan.

When it comes to banks, don't advertise. You've got two bank patrons at a local bank. One person standing in line for the teller window is holding his savings withdrawal slip in plain view. He might as well shout to everybody in the bank that he is taking a large amount of money out of his account. Right behind him is a woman with everything tucked neatly away in an envelope. The bad guy has no idea what she is going to do. He does not know if it is a deposit or a withdrawal. Which one of these two is the most vulnerable? Which one presents a target of opportunity?

The ATM

ATMs are another place you need to be a Tough Target. There's the classic case of the detective who asked the bank robber why he robbed banks? His answer: "Because that's where the money is." Well, he's right. And in most cases, when people stop at an ATM, they will walk away with some cash. So you've got to be aware of your surroundings. Never go to an ATM if you sense any kind of trouble, especially at night.

When you do use the machine, make sure no one can see you enter your personal identification number (PIN). You'd be surprised how resourceful these guys can be in accessing that number. And guess what? If he's got your number, he's going to want to have your card. So all of a sudden, you're vulnerable. You become a target of opportunity. Don't stand there and count your money.

Whatever you do, do not toss the receipt. Many banks print the account number on receipts. This is a check cloner's dream. A check cloner takes your account information and makes checks with your number on them. With checks in hand, they get very inventive in ripping you off!

It takes less than $2,000 worth of desktop publishing equipment to be in the check-cloning business. And it's a big business! Check fraud runs into the billions of dollars every year. It's the number one criminal assault on the financial system. Bank robberies, on the other hand, which attract a lot more media attention, net the bad guys around $70 million per year. A small number by comparison. So do not toss that receipt!

If you are in your car and approach a drive-up ATM window, the same rules apply. But you need to be even more careful here because these drive-up windows may be at the rear of the bank, or some other secluded area.

Secluded areas are the turf of the bad guys. And they love to play the game on their own turf. So be careful and remember, when you're in your car keep the doors locked and the windows up at all times. Then if the bad guy comes out from behind a pillar and surprises you, at least he's not going to jump in the backseat of your car and point a gun to your head. And if he does surprise you, drive away!

Chapter 5

EXERCISING
IN SAFETY

If you exercise outdoors regularly, you've probably heard all the basics: Don't run after dark, don't wear headphones, don't run alone. These factors are all important. And when it comes to your safety, these rules apply in "safe" neighborhoods too. You can't be lulled into a false sense of security just because you live on a neat, tree-lined street. You do not need to be afraid to go outside and exercise. You've got to be taught to do certain things and use certain skills if a bad situation presents itself. This stuff can happen, and I know how to prevent it. You'll be more self-assured, which will be apparent in how you look and carry yourself.

Here are some tips:

- Wear a fanny pack. Keep a canister of pepper spray and a personal alarm inside it. I suggest you also carry an ID and a small amount of cash in case of an emergency.

- Earphones are not smart. It's like wearing sunglasses in the dark. I realize lots of people love them. In fact, I've had people say to me, "But I feel so confident when I'm listening to my own music." Well, that's because music is blocking out reality. Since you can't hear what's going on around you, you may not have that extra three- or four-yard warning you need to break away. Or give him a shot of pepper spray, or avoid some out-of-control roller-blader. My advice to you—lose the headphones.

- If you can, team up with a friend. The bad guys typically go for the lone target. And if you're a runner, that friend can be your dog! Goofs definitely do not like dogs. What's the best time to exercise outdoors? The early-morning hours when the bad guys are still in bed.

- In terms of clothing, sheer can equal fear. Exercise gear has evolved from heavy, baggy sweatpants and sweatshirts to light, form-fitting tights and tops. The problem is that the latter may invite the wrong kind of attention. Of course, you have the right to wear whatever you want. But consider this: If two women

---

are running side by side, one with baggy sweats and the other with flashy skin-fitting tights, the woman who is wearing less may not feel as confident because she is revealing more of her body.

Because she may feel more vulnerable, she may look away or down at her feet when people approach. Remember, these are signs a bad guy looks for when he evaluates how vulnerable someone is. If you want to wear more revealing clothing, then it's up to you to be more alert to what's going on around you. You will attract attention—some good and some bad—so you've got to look tough to discourage the attention you don't want. Maybe you want to save the tight-fitting clothing for the gym and wear less-revealing clothes on the street. I have a T-shirt with "Northside Homicide" on it. My daughter wears it when she exercises. Believe me, it works!

Personal Defense Tools

There are two factors—other than training—that are important in personal defense sprays. The first is the distance at which it can be used. The second is the duration of the spray.

DISTANCE: It doesn't matter what type of dispenser is used as long as the product can be used close-up. A properly designed personal defense spray has no minimum required distance to prevent injury. You should be able to spray an assailant directly in the face even at point-blank range and get full effect without doing permanent damage to the assailant's eyes.

In terms of maximum distance, six to eight feet is a good distance. Anything beyond that is probably not realistic given the nature of most attacks.

DURATION OF SPRAY: Since you don't want to run out of spray before you run out of confrontation, there should be a minimum of ten seconds of total continuous discharge when you press the actuator.

There are two general classes of personal defense sprays. The first is tear gas; the second is aerosol subject restraints (ASRs) or pepper sprays.

Tear Gas

Everyone has heard of tear gas. Some tear gas sprays contain CN, which works by causing pain. They work quickly, but often someone highly enraged, psychotic, or on drugs or alcohol will be resistant to pain. You're not likely to find a product that contains only CN, but if you do don't buy it.

Another type of tear gas contains CS. It causes the eyes to close, produces heavy tearing, coughing, a feeling of panic, disorientation, and confusion. A well-formulated CS will work virtually all the time, even on pain-resistant attackers. It can, however, take twenty to sixty seconds for the full effect to kick in, making some formulations inappropriate for spontaneous defense. Another minus is that most CS defense sprays are packaged in canisters that shoot the product out in a narrow stream. This may require a minimum safe distance for spraying, something you definitely do not want.

Pepper Spray

Capsaicin-based products are inflammatory agents, and work by inflaming the mucous membranes. They are made from red peppers similar to hot peppers used in cooking. This is important because inflammation of tissues is a very low-level physiological response, unaffected by factors such as stress, drugs, alcohol, psychosis, or any other form of pain resistance. So if you spray someone who is intoxicated or on drugs, the pepper spray will still work for you.

If you buy a quality pepper spray, it is nonflammable, nontoxic, and nonlethal. It is portable and it's effective. I recommend a pepper spray over personal safety sprays that contain tear gas or a hybrid blend of tear gas and pepper spray. The reason is simple—pepper sprays work better and have proven superior to tear gases in controlling persons under the influence of alcohol or illegal drugs.

Once you get the right stuff, what happens if you're in trouble and you spray the bad guy? Well, the results are instantaneous. The pepper spray will incapacitate an attacker for up to twenty minutes, but causes no permanent damage.

I suggest you purchase at least a couple of different models. One is a half-ounce model that is designed to be carried right on your key ring; the other, a three-ounce police model, can be kept in your glove compartment or home. The delivery mechanism is also important, so be sure to ask about that as well. Try practicing with an inert training unit filled with sterile water. Your reflexes need to be quick—so don't hesitate.

Your life may be riding on your ability to use this weapon, so you need to know its capabilities. Make sure the unit is accessible as well. It won't do you much good if it's not. When you walk to your car, have your keys—and pepper spray—in hand. That automatically makes you a tougher target. In some states there are certain restrictions on carrying a pepper spray, so check with local authorities.

- Spray the bad guy. That will stop him in his tracks. The most important tactic is to create and maintain distance. Spray and keep spraying, following the movement of his face.
- Shout verbal commands. The bad guy is not going to just stand there and let you spray him. Shout DOWN! DOWN! DOWN! Second, scream bloody murder—FIRE! FIRE! FIRE!—to attract attention.
- Get out of there as fast as you can.

A quality pepper spray will incapacitate an attacker for up to twenty minutes, but causes no permanent damage.

The Personal Alarm

We already know that sound is an effective, nonviolent method of self-defense. A personal alarm can help you to attract attention in a compromising situation. It is a simple, inexpensive device that works. It is about the same size as a beeper. When in danger, you pull a pin to emit a distinct piercing noise to ward off potential attackers. This noise will create enough of a distraction for you to escape and bring help to the scene.

Advantages:

- An alarm is nonaggressive and cannot be turned against the user; yet the alarm is assertive and sends a clear message that you have no intention of being victimized.
- Sound can be used earlier in a threatening situation than most other options.
- There is little training needed.
- An alarm is also quite versatile. It is compact, lightweight, and can be easily clipped to a belt or purse. How can this help you? Let's say you have the alarm inside your purse and the cord—which is attached to the pin—is within your grasp. If a bad guy comes out of the alley and grabs your purse, it may be on its way off your shoulder but you can still grab the pin, and suddenly this guy is running down the street with a purse that sounds like a fire truck.

In addition, many alarms come with a special adapter enabling them to serve as door or window alarms. This is ideal for travel, for women or seniors living alone, or for those without a home security system! If there is an attempt to open the door or window, the alarm goes off.

It's great to have alarms and sprays, but the best help we can get comes from the people around us.

CAROLE AND LEROY

On a crisp, clear February evening in 1993, Carole Pooler arrived home from her job and headed out for her nightly jog. At fifty-one, she was in better shape than most women half her age. Carole consistently ran forty miles a week. Always alone. Never in fear.

Carole loved to jog along Chicago's beautiful lakefront, and each evening she made the short drive from her home to Grant Park, which is adjacent to the lake. A few miles away, thirty-eight-year-old cab driver Leroy Montgomery—a father of five—was nearing the end of a long shift. He was a veteran of the streets and one of Yellow Cab Company's most popular and respected drivers. He liked the job and took pride in his work.

Back in the park, Carole was beginning to really get into her run. She had no idea that just ahead, hiding in a small clump of trees, were two young hoodlums carrying knives. These thugs were out to rob the first good target that came by, and suddenly they were face-to-face with Carole. She was startled. They panicked. She didn't have a chance.

They stabbed her repeatedly in the arms and back and then, probably out of fear of being identified, tried to kill her by slitting her throat. Carole managed to scramble free and the boys fled in the opposite direction. They didn't get any money from Carole because she wasn't carrying any.

Meanwhile Carole, bleeding profusely, mustered up every ounce of strength she had and managed to stumble up an embankment to street level. Delirious and in shock, she wandered aimlessly onto busy Lakeshore Drive. Cars were flying by in every direction, many honking their horns and yelling out their windows, thinking this had to be some kind of crazy woman!

As Carole struggled to stay on her feet and avoid being hit by passing cars, Leroy was nearby. He recognized the situation for what it was, slammed on his brakes, and jumped out of his cab. He got to Carole just as she collapsed. As the traffic became more congested, Leroy then noticed the seriousness of her wounds. Knowing there was no time to wait for an ambulance, Leroy propped Carole up right on the street and, as gently as possible, placed her in his cab. He instructed her to put pressure on her neck wound and then sped off to the hospital, not sure if he would make it in time to save Carole's life.

Fortunately, he did. Carole's injuries were severe, and she was rushed into emergency surgery. Thanks to her stamina, a strong will to live, and a very unassuming hero, she survived.

Carole couldn't comprehend what was happening to her at the time and thought, I'm never going to see my grandchildren again. Then she knew she had to fight back. Fortunately, she managed to break free, and when she stumbled out onto to Lakeshore Drive, her guardian angel, Leroy, was there. There is no question that he saved her life.

A year and a half before this incident, Leroy held his dying son in his arms. Seventeen-year-old Derek Montgomery was beaten to death on the street by a group of teens in a random act of violence.

At an awards ceremony, Leroy was named International Cab Driver of the Year. In his acceptance speech, he spoke of the senseless murder of his son and his harrowing experience with Carole. "No one came to help my son, and I vowed I would not let that happen to someone else. I also vowed that I was not going to let his death change me for the worse. I decided it would change me for the better. So often people witness violence and they just walk away. Well, my advice is this: Be a part of the solution, not part of the problem. My advice is, get involved."

Chapter 6

AVOIDING SECLUDED PLACES

Part of being a Tough Target means being smart. Don't put yourself in compromising situations or places. You're only asking for trouble.

DANA FEITLER

Dana was a smart, talented twenty-four-year-old woman. A beautiful person in every sense of the word! Dana had decided to return to school after working in a bank for two years. She was joined by two friends for dinner and drinks to celebrate her acceptance into the University of Chicago's prestigious MBA program.

It was a rainy night in June, about one A.M., when they decided to call it a night. Dana was dropped off at the front door of her apartment building by one of her friends. They said good night and waved to each other as he pulled away. Dana then went into the vestibule of her apartment building located in the exclusive Gold Coast area. She stopped to pick up her mail and suddenly—out of nowhere—she was confronted by two men. One of the men put a gun to her head and demanded her money. You can guess the line: "Give us your money, lady, and we're outta here. Nobody's going to get hurt. Just do as I say."

Dana had no cash in her purse but she did have a bank card. The two men then forced her out of the building and into their car. At this point, they were joined by another man, who had been acting as a lookout. They drove to a nearby ATM, where Dana withdrew two hundred dollars. This did not satisfy her captors, so they drove her around for a short time and then forced her to withdraw another two hundred dollars.

On the second trip to the ATM, a woman walking her dog noticed Dana with the three men and thought something was suspicious. She even exchanged glances with Dana. But she shrugged it off and went on her way.

After the second withdrawal, the three men walked her into an alley. The guy with the weapon forced her to her knees, put the gun to the back of her head execution style, and pulled the trigger. After five days in a coma, Dana died.

This tragedy wasn't Dana's fault. She didn't know what to do in this situation. Let's retrace her steps and look at what happened here, so if you find yourself in a similar situation you do know what to do. A friend dropped her off in front of her apartment building. Should he have waited until she was safely inside the building? Yes, absolutely!

These guys were lurking about, waiting for the right target. Dana walked in alone, the coast was clear, and they were ready to strike. Chances are she never had a chance to get beyond the lobby area and into a secure part of the building. Once these guys made their move, it's a rough situation there in the lobby. There's not much anybody can do there.

Outside is a different story. Outside there are people. If you're outside you can attract attention. Sure, you're scared—after all, this guy has a gun. But you need to keep your wits about you because that's your only chance to survive. You've got to be prepared.

It's about having a plan. And if you can't make your move right away, as in this case, look for an opening as soon as you can. Look for a chance to break and run.

For Dana, that opportune moment to run may have come just as they exited the building or at the ATM. Or when the woman with the dog showed up on the scene. Anything that distracts the goofs from their mission is an opportunity for you to escape. And the woman with the dog was a distraction. So there's your opening. If this guy has your arm, give him an elbow with all you've got and spin away from his grasp. Then run like hell, yelling FIRE! FIRE! FIRE!

We've got to help one another out. Should the woman walking the dog have trusted her instincts? Of course. She sensed trouble but ignored those instincts. You can't do that. Get to a phone, call 911, flag down a police car, or yell, "I'm calling the police," even if you don't have a cellular phone. Because he doesn't know if you do or if you don't, and they can't take that chance.

If you are running down the street yelling FIRE! and there's someone else on the street yelling, "I'm calling the police," what is the goof going to do? Well, there's a good chance he won't do anything except get out of there himself. And if he does fire the weapon, chances are he's going to hesitate. That hesitation puts you thirty feet away and he's probably a lousy shot anyway. Your odds of surviving just went up. If you go down that alley with this guy, what are your odds then? Zero.

• If you drop someone off at a home or apartment, wait until that person is safely inside before leaving.

- Be aware of your surroundings at all times.
- Carry a container of pepper spray on your key ring and be sure it is visible. That alone makes you a tougher target.
- Help one another out. Create a distraction if you see someone in trouble.
- If you are confronted, give up the property and get out of there. Do not wait around for request number two.
- Never, ever let them take you to a private place.

Stairwells and Elevators

Stairwells are even simpler: Stay out! Unless it is an emergency. If you want some exercise, go to the gym or go for a walk. Stairwells are, by law, fireproof, and very little noise comes out of that space. So if you get caught in a stairwell, you're trapped.

Let's take a solo ride on an elevator. You're on the elevator, it stops, and the door opens. If someone gets on you don't like, get off. Say, "Excuse me, my floor!" and you're out of there.

How long will you have to wait for the next elevator? A minute? Maybe two? Isn't that wait worth avoiding potential trouble? Same thing if you're waiting for the elevator: It stops and you don't like who's on that elevator—don't get on. It's as simple as that.

But sometimes it isn't quite that simple. This time you're on the elevator, the door opens, and the guy that hops on looks okay. The doors close and now you're alone with this guy. Well, you're smart, so you stand next to the buttons. And if he confronts you, push all the buttons except the button that stops the elevator. It's usually red!

He wants that elevator stopped mid-floor, but you don't. You want to keep it moving. Every time that door opens there's a chance for you to escape. Every time that door opens there's a chance for you to get help. And if he does manage to push the stop button, you've got to pull it out. Here fleeing isn't an option. So you need to be prepared to fight this guy to keep that elevator moving.

Consider this: One woman fights this guy and scrambles off the elevator to safety. She takes a punch in the face in the process. Maybe she gets a broken nose. Another woman lets this guy stop the elevator and she is raped. One of these women will heal. The other may never heal. Which one would you want to be?

What do you do if you're standing there, the door opens, and inside some goof is attacking a woman on the elevator? Do you try to fight him off or grab her? Well, it's the latter. If you go for him, he's going to fight you. If you go for her, she's going to work with you. So try to pull her away from this guy and off the elevator. Chances are he'll make a run for it anyway.

What did Elane Crosby learn from her ordeal? Her response was simply this: "Have a plan. And don't ever go to the secondary crime scene."

- Stairwells: Stay out of stairwells unless it's an emergency.
- Elevators: Avoid being alone on an elevator with someone you're uncomfortable with. If you do get confronted, push all the buttons and be prepared to fight the attacker to keep the elevator running.

BOOK II

Chapter 7

PROTECTING YOUR CHILDREN

There is nothing more important than the safety of our children. They're our responsibility and our legacy. Children are our future. We need to provide our children with the tools they need to grow and develop into responsible adults. This requires a team effort on the part of parents, teachers, and the community. We need to make our children Tough Targets.

At a minimum, we must guarantee that all children learn and play in safe schools and neighborhoods. Unfortunately, that's not the case in far too many places. There are no safe havens for many children. They are victimized at home, at school, and on the street. In December of 1995, a children's advocacy group released the results of a national survey. Seventy-one percent of the children questioned, between the ages of seven and ten, said that they worried that they might get shot or stabbed at school or at home.

Today our children are facing an epidemic of violent crime that is sweeping the country. Much is written about guns and gangs and ghettos. But this onslaught of childhood violence knows no boundaries of race, geography, or class. And it's time we turn this around. We've got to instill in our children confidence that adults can protect them and keep them safe. We've got to address violence against our kids the way we treat other public health threats like drunken driving or drug abuse—we must focus our efforts on safety education and violence prevention.

There are many people who, like myself, are committed to turning this epidemic around. But many more are needed. It's a big job, but we can get it done.

I've investigated many, many cases of child rape and murder. I've arrested and interrogated child killers and I've testified in court at their trials, I've been at their sentencings. It takes a lot of control to do the investigation and not throw the pervert out of the window. You carry the grief and rage with you always. I try to channel it to do some good. I remember that every day. That's why I try to inform and instruct the people how to prevent these crimes from occurring in their community.

I remember one eleven-year-old girl who was found dead in an abandoned building. She was brought to the morgue and examined by a pathologist. The cause of death was listed as manual strangulation. This means that she was choked to death with bare hands. But when I looked at the body, lying on the stainless-steel gurney in the morgue, I saw her neck covered with bruises—I could see the killer's handprints on her little neck. This indicated which way the child was lying when she was killed. From the location of these bruises and the visible thumbprints of the killer—I knew exactly what had happened. This innocent little girl was lying on her back when she was killed. The last thing on earth this child did as she took her last breath was look into the face of this guy as he strangled the life out of her body.

No one should ever have to look at a body like that. I don't want that nightmare to happen to your family. Do whatever it takes to protect your children from these guys. It's so much easier to plan ahead and keep your family safe.

Preventing Child Abduction

The very thought of someone taking your child sends chills down the spine of every parent. Just like the whereabouts of thousands of missing children, the number of child abductions each year is a mystery.

A recent Justice Department study found there are approximately 360,000 child abductions annually. The vast majority—about 355,000—are abductions by family members, which are usually related to custody disputes.

Of the 5,000 or so abductions unrelated to family feuds, about 300 involve the kidnapping or murder of a child. There is no way to tell how many attempts there are. These near misses are attempted abductions that are never reported or reported after the fact and never become official. Let's examine the 300 that we do know about. It is these cases that often gain national media coverage. It is these cases the public finds most terrifying.

Keep in mind that 300 may not seem a very high number to most people but when we're talking about your children, even one abduction is too many.

POLLY KLAAS

Polly Klaas was abducted in the bedroom of her Petaluma, California, home. Her picturesque town had always been described as a wonderful place to raise children. "Stay with us and listen to the grapes grow" was the slogan of a nearby bed-and-breakfast.

One night in October, a stranger crept into the bedroom of twelve-year-old Polly. He held a knife to Polly's throat, forced her out the unlocked back door, through which he had entered, and took her away forever.

A frenzied search ensued, a search that seemed to epitomize the nation's anguish over crime. Two months later, Richard Allen Davis, a career criminal, was brought into custody. He admitted to kidnapping Polly and led investigators to her body. The outrage in this peaceful community was understandable. Killers like Davis affect whole communities and steal their sense of peace and security forever. The mayor of Petaluma said, "We were a small town, or we thought we were. A lot of people did not lock their houses at night. That now has changed. Now they lock up their houses."

Think of how easy it is. A simple precaution such as locking the back door can keep your family safe.

STEPHANIE CRANE

Nine-year-old Stephanie Crane loved to ride her bike, fish with her dad, and hang out with her friends. It was a cool and sunny day in October and Stephanie was excited about attending the birthday party of a good friend. Stephanie's mother, Sandy, buttoned her daughter's sweater and sent her on her way. She didn't give it a second thought. After all, it was just a few blocks to Challis Lanes Entertainment Center, where the party was being held.

It was a fun afternoon. Stephanie and her friends had a great time bowling, eating cake, and talking about boys. When the party ended midafternoon, Stephanie said goodbye to her friends and headed back home. That was the last time she was seen.

When Stephanie's mother realized her daughter was missing, she called the police immediately. Within minutes, over 250 volunteers were on the scene. The entire town turned out to help in the search and provide support. Everyone was aware of how critical the first twenty-four hours are in any abduction and Sandy was hopeful.

Despite the intensive search, Stephanie has not come back. She remains missing to this day. Stephanie's mother is still hopeful that one day her daughter will return and put their lives back in order.

SARA ANNE WOOD

On August 18, 1993, twelve-year-old Sara, a cheerleader at school, was riding her bike home from the church where her father is pastor. It is just down a country road, about a half-mile away. She never made it. A short time later, Lewis S. Lent, Jr., was arrested and linked to the abduction and murder of Sara. Despite a massive search in upstate New York, her body was never found.

Six month's after her abduction, Sara's father, Bob, described the nightmare:

"The worst possible thing that can happen to anyone is not knowing where your child is, especially when that child is young and innocent, as my daughter Sara was. It's like someone comes along and steals part of your life away from you. It's almost like ripping a part of your heart right out of your chest. This has been a horrendous experience.

"And it's not over yet. We're still trying to find my daughter's body. They're digging in the snow—I've been up there digging in the snow—because we believe she's buried in a shallow grave somewhere up north. For months I didn't want to believe it. But now, based on the evidence of the state police, I believe she's gone.

"Not knowing where your child is is like an open hole that drains the life right out of you. It takes enormous energy to get up and face the day. The longer the process goes on, the worse it gets.

"I thank God for the time my wife and I had with Sara, because every day is precious. You may not lose your child to a stranger on the road—it might be a car accident or illness. You just never know. So my advice to parents is this: Spend time with your kids. Talk to them. Love them every day. I used to talk to Sara each night. I still do. I go to her room and I kneel and pray. And even though I know her body is destroyed, her spirit lives on."

Reacting to the Lure

Many child abductions begin with "the lure." If it's an older child, around twelve, it's usually the opportunity to make a quick buck. The guy will tell the child that he has a bad back and will offer to pay five dollars to help load some boxes into his van or the trunk of his car. Five minutes for five bucks. Not a bad deal. This offer will sound appealing to most kids—but it's deadly. The child will be pushed into a van and taken on a one-way trip.

With younger children, it's a different lure, usually candy, help with directions, or the lost puppy. In one appearance on *The Jerry Springer Show*, we performed an experiment. With the permission and cooperation of several mothers, they hired an actor and set up a hidden camera to see if their children could be lured away by a stranger.

The actor was Jerry Spiwak. Jerry is a very distinguished-looking gentleman; he could be your local bank president, insurance agent, or even your dentist. The children were left by their mothers to play together in a suburban playground. The playground was located in a large park surrounded by a forest preserve. It was cold and the ground was covered with snow. All the children, ranging between ages four and seven, were bundled up. Jerry was dressed in a heavy brown winter coat, a hat, jeans, and boots. He looked anything but menacing. He looked like a grandfather!

Here's what happened when he approached the children:

JERRY: "Hi. I lost my dog Harvey. He's a little black poodle, have you seen him?"

CHILD ONE: No.

JERRY: Will you help me find him?

CHILD ONE: Okay.

JERRY: I lost him over this way.

HE POINTS AND THEY BEGIN TO WALK TOGETHER IN THE OPPOSITE DIRECTION.

JERRY: I'll give you some candy.

CHILD ONE: I don't need any.

JERRY: You don't need any? Okay. I'll let you pet him when we find him then. C'mon, let's go.

A FEW MORE CHILDREN JOIN IN THE SEARCH.

CHILD TWO: Which way did you come into the park?

JERRY: I came in over there, by the bushes.

CHILD TWO: Is that where you live?

JERRY: Yeah. Do you live around here?

CHILD TWO: I live in Willowbrook.

JERRY: Willowbrook, huh? Where's your mother?

CHILD TWO: I don't know. She's probably over there somewhere.

JERRY: Okay, we'll stop and visit her later.

THE THREE OF THEM ARE NOW MOVING CLOSER TO THE WOODED AREA ADJACENT TO THE PARK.

CHILD ONE: Were you playing in the park with your dog?

JERRY: Yeah, I came into the park with my dog and I lost him.

CHILD THREE: What did he look like?

JERRY: He's a black poodle and his name is Harvey.

NOW, TO THE HORROR OF THE PARENTS WATCHING NEARBY, JERRY BEGINS TO MOVE EVEN CLOSER TO THE WOODED AREA, WITH THE KIDS FOLLOWING RIGHT BEHIND HIM.

CHILD TWO: Where did he run away to?

JERRY: Well, he ran this way. Toward the bushes here.

THE OTHER TWO KIDS THEN JOIN IN THE PROCESSION. THEY WALK ON, THIS MAN AND THE FIVE LITTLE CHILDREN. OUT OF THE PARK AND INTO THE WOODS . . .

JERRY: The first one who finds him gets a reward!

Two of the mothers were in the audience that day and watched this scenario unfold. They were horrified! Both mothers had talked to their children about strangers and thought the children understood. "My daughter's innocence took over and she forgot all that she had learned. She said he was such a sweet man."

The other mother said that she had talked to her child about strangers and even role-played certain scenarios with her, including the lost dog con. During the role playing, her daughter screamed and ran away. Why didn't she do that in this situation? The man managed to get her trust in such a short period of time. When this situation was being set up the mother said, "There's no way that Kimberly will go. She'll run the other way and yell." But Kimberly just followed along with the others. The "abductor" did manage to gain the trust of these kids right away. And that's what these guys do. And they're very good at it. The first thing you need to do is to make sure the children understand that the bad guys look like normal people. **The bad guys don't all look like Charles Manson or Freddie Krueger or Bluto. They look like fathers and uncles and grandfathers and neighbors because they *are* fathers and uncles and grandfathers and neighbors.**

This can be a very tough concept to communicate to a young child. If the bad guy is a nice man and he's lost his puppy, shouldn't the child help him out? And sometimes what appears to be a stranger to the parent is not a stranger to the child. These guys will hang out around schools and playgrounds and make friends with the kids, so then they're not strangers. What can you teach your child so they don't fall for something like this?

Teaching Your Child

Here's what we can do to communicate the message without making our kids paranoid. Kimberly's mother said she used role playing to make the point about strangers, and that's a good start. But I suggest taking it one step further. Set up a scenario where you have a "stranger" approach the child with a lure or by asking directions. Maybe you can do this when your child is out bike riding. Choose someone you know but the child doesn't.

Watch and see what happens. That's your real test. That will tell you if your child has grasped the concept of stranger-danger.

Yell Stranger!

Teach your children that they must never speak to an adult they don't know. An adult will always beat your child in a match of wits.

When you teach your child these guidelines, he or she will often say, "Mommy, you talk to strangers." Your reply could be this: "Yes, I do talk to strangers; I also drive a car and vote and do other adult things. When you become an adult you can too." This concept is easy to understand. Gradually, as the children get older, they get more freedom from the parent.

Here is another example of this concept. When you first cross a street with a child, you will hold onto the child's hand and you will not let go until you have reached the safety of the other side. As the child gets older you will hold their hand less frequently. Sometimes you let the child hold onto your coat if your hands are full. The child learns and gets experience at the side of the parent. When the child is older they will be able to cross the street alone. The child was taught by example. It's the same as talking to strangers.

If your child is ever approached by someone that they do not know, they should yell NO! and get away. No hesitation—it's NO! and they're out of there. And while the child is running away they should be yelling Stranger! Real loud! At the top of their little lungs. Over and over again.

Stranger is one word that is poison to the bad guys' ears because it gets an immediate reaction, and gets others involved. Consider this scenario: A child is abducted from inside a mall and this kid is resisting, perhaps crying and trying to break free. Is that enough? No, because we see parents struggling with tired and cranky kids all the time. So this behavior might be ignored by others. And that gives the bad guy the opportunity to get that child out of the mall and into the parking lot. And we know that at that point, it's all over. If that same child is crying, trying to break free, and yelling Stranger! Stranger! Stranger! that's a different story. People will get involved because stranger is the only word that will get every adult to look at the kid and help out.

The most important thing you can do for a child is empower the child to say no to an adult. If you teach the child that it's okay to say no to an adult, they will use this if a compromising situation ever arises. This is especially important in the area of forced affection. Here's a scenario that we have all probably been guilty of at one time.

PARENT: Grandpa's leaving, go give him a big kiss.

CHILD: Daddy, I don't want to kiss Grandpa.

PARENT: Hey, that was a nice birthday present he just gave you. Go give him a big hug and a kiss.

CHILD: I don't want to kiss Grandpa. His breath smells funny.

PARENT: Hey, that's my father, now you get in there and you kiss him goodbye.

Well, the lesson that was just taught to this child at a very young and impressionable age is that the child has no control over the affection that's forced on them. The child was just taught that adults are allowed to force affection on them and they have nothing to say about it. That's wrong! It's wrong for the child and it's wrong for the parents. The child should do whatever they feel comfortable with, maybe a high five, handshake, wave, hug, or kiss. That way, when grandpa gets a kiss, he knows it's from the heart and it's not just an outward sign forced by the parents. But more important, the child is comfortable with the level of affection and has made the decision on their own.

When you give the choice back to the child, then the child is tough and knows that it's okay to say No!

This really works. Then when the child is five years old and "Uncle Bob" or "Mr. Jones" wants to take this kid into the next room to play a "secret game," this kid is not going to go. And when the little girl is fifteen, and she's involved in a date rape situation, she'll be tough because all of her life her mother and father have told her, if you don't want to be kissed or touched or hugged, then no one touches you. Don't send any mixed signals to your children. If your son or daughter is encouraged to say no to forced affection from their own family, they'll say no to anybody!

STRANGER IN A CAR

What if your child is approached by someone asking directions from a car?

Well, as soon as someone asks a child for directions, you know this is a scam; men never ask directions. Why would someone who is old enough to have a driver's license ask a ten-year-old for directions? So what does the child do? The child runs in the opposite direction from where the car is heading. Why? Because by the time this guy can turn the car around that kid is gone and is yelling STRANGER!

What do you think the bad guy is going to do? He's going to get out of there and look for someone else's kid, some kid who is not a Tough Target.

Drop the Books

What happens if the child is carrying a book bag and they're trying to run away from a bad guy? The weight will slow them down. So what's the solution? Tell the child to drop the books! But make sure there are no mixed messages! Most parents have told their son or daughter not to leave their book bag on the bus, or at the library or at their friend's house, to avoid having to buy another set of books. The parent has put the fear of God in their child. The child knows if they come home without their books there will be real trouble.

One little girl was taken into an alley and was fondled by some creep. I witnessed the police report as she told her father, "Daddy, I almost got away, but that book bag was so heavy."

The parent had reinforced the wrong thing. If the child drops the books and runs away, that is good. If you get back there and the books are gone, that's okay too. Book bags and supplies can be replaced.

Adults should give their purse or wallet to a bad guy and a child should drop their books. It's called "taking a draw." You give up a little to save a lot. The bad guy is not after this kid's spelling homework, book bag, or new crayons. He wants the child!

This same principle applies if the child is grabbed on the street. If someone grabs the child's coat, or backpack, or sweatshirt, they should try to get free from the clothing or backpack and run. You have to tell your kids to RUN. The kids watch shows like *Ninja Turtles* and *Power Rangers* and they can get the idea that they are invincible and can fight the bad guys. The child says to their mom, "Mommy, if they ever come after me, I'm gonna get them." And the kid gets into a karate stance. Well, you've got a forty-pound kid up against a 200-pound man. Who's going to win? You have to make sure they remember to run—not stay and fight.

REBECCA SAVARESE

On a cold, snowy day, twelve-year-old Becky came face-to-face with one of her worst nightmares. A guy just came up behind her and said, "Do you see the gun I have? Do everything I say and it will be all right."

They walked up to where his truck was parked and he told her to get into the truck. Rebecca was very smart and started to fake an asthma attack. She sat down and he tried to grab her but he only got hold of her backpack. When he did that, Rebecca ran away down the street. She knew if she went into the truck she wouldn't come out. She was right. The guy turned out to be Lewis Lent, Jr., killer of Sara Anne Wood.

Safety in Numbers

Teach your child to travel a specified and safe route to and from school or the park. They should also be taught never to take shortcuts and to always walk with a friend—never alone. In over ninety percent of child abductions the bad guy takes one child, rarely two, and never three. Children need to stick together. There is safety in numbers. A great example of sticking together is apparent in the movie *Top Gun*, the most important thing the pilots are taught is never to leave your wing-man! The movie illustrates that two planes flying together are much more powerful than two planes flying apart. In Scuba diving the same rule applies. Two divers swimming together are safer than two divers swimming and exploring on their own.

I also like to use another analogy to explain this principle to children. When the Navy wants to move a bunch of ships from one place to another, it moves them in a group called a fleet. This fleet of ships travels together. They have a unique plan: They move at the fastest speed of the slowest ship. That's the safest and most effective way to accomplish the mission. The same goes for your kids. Their mission is to arrive safely at their destination. So tell your children to walk with at least one friend. If there is a group of children, they need to walk at the fastest speed of the slowest child.

The next story is a classic example of how kids can stick together.

CAMERON NOEL

When Cameron was ten years old he would always walk to school with his friends Ernie, Gabrielle, and Terry. One day they saw a car driving down the wrong side of the street. A man got out of the car, opened the back door, and sat down. The kids had no idea what he was doing. When they got closer to the car, he jumped out and grabbed Ernie. The guy put his hand over Ernie's mouth, threw him in the backseat of his car, and then closed the door. Cameron told Gabrielle and Terry to run for help and then went right up to the car. He kicked the abductor right between the legs. When that happened, the guy fell down and Cameron opened up the back door to let his friend free. Cameron carried Ernie from the scene on his back. Then they ran toward school while the men drove off.

With Gabrielle's description, a neighbor searched the streets, found the suspect, and blocked his exit from a driveway long enough for the police to arrive. The abductor was arrested and charged with kidnapping. Cameron's friend Ernie was the youngest of the group and yet the group stayed together and helped each other. Had Cameron and the others been a half-block ahead of Ernie, chances are he would have become another statistic.

Ignore the Gun

For years people have been taught that if someone threatens them with a gun they should give up everything. This is true, but some forget to mention to their child that they must run away as fast as they can. The bad guy is not going to shoot the child right there in broad daylight on the street. Tell this to your child. The gun only serves as a tool to intimidate the child. These predators do not want a dead body lying on the side of the road. They want that live child sitting beside them in the car, or in the van, or in the truck. So kids must ignore the gun, ignore the threat, and run!

It's important to give your child instructions on where to run. But keep it simple. Something like this: "If you are not past Main Street, run home. If you are past Main Street, run to school. Or run to a fast-food restaurant. Run anywhere where there are people."

Using a Personal Alarm

The personal alarm is a great tool for kids as well as adults. Clip the alarm to the child's clothing or book bag and be sure to put an identifying label on it. Be sure to include your name and phone number. If the child is abducted and the alarm is left behind, the police will know who to call. You can then give a description of the child so the police know who they are looking for.

Using a Password

What happens if there is an emergency situation and you need to have someone who your child doesn't know pick them up from school? Your child has been taught not to go anywhere with strangers but this is a special circumstance. Well, a bad guy knows that in an emergency the normal rules do not apply, so he tells your child that Mom has had a serious car accident and he's there to take them to the hospital. Well, we certainly do not want the child getting into the car with some creep, and we do not want the child standing on the corner waiting two hours for a parent who was really involved in an accident.

To prepare for emergencies, parents and children should decide on a password that will be used when you need to have an adult who the child doesn't know pick up the child from school or a neighbor's house. The unknown adult meets your child and says, "Your mother told me to say 'Blue Buffalo.'" Now the child knows that this person was really sent by their mom or dad. And they know that it is okay to get into the car with this stranger.

The password is a simple solution. Choose a password with two words that don't normally go together. For example, Blue Buffalo or Green Sky. Don't let the child select the password. If you let the kid pick, they usually want Barney or one of the Ninja Turtles, or whatever is in style at the time—and this is something a bad guy might figure out.

Responding to Abductions

What happens if your child is abducted? Here are some important facts that you need to know: The first twenty-four hours are critical. Call the police immediately. They will set up a command center, begin the investigation, and organize the search. And this really does require organization because it often involves hundreds of volunteers and they need leadership and direction to be effective. The police may also call on other law enforcement agencies to assist in the investigation, including the FBI.

The FBI's Rapid Start team is a valuable resource that can move quickly. Rapid Start is a computer database program that allows local agencies to pinpoint the most promising leads. This program can access the FBI technology centers in Montana, Idaho, Georgia, and Washington, D.C. The leads can then be cross-referenced with other cases in the national database.

Here's how Don Vilfer of the FBI describes it: "Rapid Start simply comes in and takes the information that's been gathered through those traditional investigative techniques—such as interviews, witness observations, calls in to hotlines —and we take all of that information and put it into our system.

"We then analyze it and attempt to assist the investigators to focus their investigation where it would be most productive. We can provide the lead-tracking mechanism to simply organize the leads and key in on those leads that appear to be most promising."

John Walsh: A Children's Crusader

Civilian John Walsh has helped to capture more criminals than any cop in this country by turning personal anger and tragedy into positive action. On July 27, 1981, John's son Adam, age 6, was shopping with his mother at a Sears store near the family's Hollywood, Florida, home. Adam went to play in the toy department and in less than ten minutes had vanished into thin air. Two weeks later, the Walshes received the grim news. Two fishermen found a child's head in a canal in Vero Beach, Florida, 120 miles north of Hollywood. Dental records confirmed that it was Adam.

John and his wife were devastated beyond belief. Despite John's anger and pain, he began a mission to ensure that Adam did not die in vain. In 1982, John gave up his job as a hotel executive to lobby full time for the passage of an act that mandates immediate investigation of any child reported missing. In 1984, another bill backed by Walsh established the nonprofit National Center for Missing and Exploited Children. By sharing its database with the FBI and police, NCMEC has helped locate more than 29,000 missing children.

John Walsh is most noted for his role as host of the long-running television series *America's Most Wanted*. Since the show's debut in 1988, viewers, responding to the cases of more than 1,000 serial killers, rapists, murderers, armed robbers, and other accused felons, have assisted in the capture of over 400 criminals, and the list is growing.

When John talks about missing children, his cool demeanor changes to one of intensity. His mission in life is to help other families avoid the grueling ordeal he had to face. Adam's killer has never been caught. "It's a wound that will never heal," he says about Adam's killing. "I don't know what I'd do if I met his killer. But I truly believe that if he isn't caught in this lifetime, he will be in the next. I'll never give up hope."

The National Center for Missing and Exploited Children's number is: 1-800-THE-LOST

Avoiding Gangs and Drugs

Child abduction is certainly one evil that steals our children. Gangs and drugs are two others that affect much larger numbers. The subjects of gangs and drugs are complex. Volumes have been written about each topic so there is no way that we can cover all the intricacies, but it's important to address them in a broad sense.

While we need to protect our children from abduction, molestation, and drugs, we also need to protect them from each other. Crimes committed by children are on the rise. The statistics of children arrested for murder increased 128 percent from 1983 to 1992. While the overall crime rate has leveled off in recent years, the number of juveniles arrested for violent crimes—rape, robbery, aggravated assault—rose 47 percent from 1988 to 1992.

Understanding Gangs

Gangs are new equal opportunity clubs. They don't discriminate against gender, age, or location. The list of do's and don'ts associated with gang life is a long one. It involves certain colors, hairstyles, hats and how they are worn, jackets, sneakers, shoelaces, and gestures. Certain driving techniques—moving fast or slow, making a sudden U-turn—can also signal gang activity. At the core of it all is the fundamental question: Why do kids join gangs?

There are three primary reasons:

- Children have no support group at home, church, and school. Many gang members come from single-parent homes, from homes where drugs are prevalent, or both.
- Intimidation is often involved. Young kids face a beating, or worse, unless they join a particular gang.
- Being a gang member offers protection from rival gangs.

It's easy to see the faulty logic in all this. The gangs create the problem on the streets in the first place and then they say they will protect their members from it. It makes no sense.

Most kids are impressionable and just want to belong. They see the gang leader driving a luxury car, wearing expensive clothes, gold chains, and Rolex watches. He's got money, status, and an arsenal of weapons. Inner city kids in gangs look at others in their neighborhood and see poverty and hopelessness. Hooking up with a gang becomes an easy decision. But it's always a bad one because once a kid joins the gang, it's a dead-end street.

There are only two ways out of a gang: the prison and the graveyard. But most kids don't understand that because the trouble usually comes later. After a kid is recruited, he is run through a progression. It goes like this: The first thing they do is give him a simple test, such as stealing from a liquor store. It seems simple enough and not too much of a risk, so the kid does it and now he's committed a crime. The gang praises him for his actions. He is taught that these activities are encouraged because they're done for the good of the gang.

Then the heat gets turned up. They set up a dope deal. The drug dealer says, "Take this paper bag and hold it. Inside are small bags of crack. When a car pulls up, I'll go talk to the driver. He'll give me the money and I'll walk away from the car. If I hold up one finger when I walk away, you go over to the car and toss one bag of dope into the car. If I hold up two fingers, you toss two bags. You hold the dope. I'll hold the money." So the dope deal goes down and now the kid has committed a very serious crime.

The crime is listed on the law books as Delivery of a Controlled Substance. Who made the delivery? Not the dealer, but the new member—the juvenile. The dealer is smart and does not want to go to jail, especially when he can get the new guy to take the bigger risk.

And then the heat gets turned up some more: "C'mon, we're just going for a ride." And the kid does as he's told because he wants to be a good soldier. He is in the middle of the backseat and he feels like part of the inner circle. They cruise the neighborhood and then some gang member pulls out a shotgun or a 9mm automatic and begins firing into a crowd of people. He's after a rival gang member and he doesn't care who gets in the way. Someone is hurt bad, maybe even dead. Our young friend is now involved in a big-time crime.

There are two ways out of the gang. One is prison.
The other is the graveyard.

The new kid—who just wanted to belong, or just wanted protection—is involved up to his eyeballs. He can be convicted of murder even though somebody else pulled the trigger. It's like the analogy of the wolfpack. It doesn't matter whether you are at the front of the pack or the back of the pack—if you're in, you're in.

Girls in Gangs

More and more girls are being recruited into gangs every day. Their motivation is basically the same as the guys and they are started out the same progressive way. The girl is told to steal some jeans from a department store. It doesn't seem like that big of a deal to her so she steals the jeans. She's the hero of the hour. And now she's in.

Now this young girl, maybe fourteen years old, starts hanging around with the gang and it seems pretty exciting to her. Then she's ordered to sleep with some guy she doesn't even know. She's trying to be cool but she doesn't want any part of this. She's told, "Hey, that's not your choice anymore. You sleep with this guy now or we'll beat hell out of you and you can sleep with him then." And the threat is real. That's what they do. They use and abuse the girls.

Gangs Are in Cities and Suburbs

Gangs were once confined primarily to the inner city—not anymore. In Springfield, Missouri, population 135,000, police arrested eighteen-year-old Marvin Herron and confiscated a .38-caliber revolver. They were shocked at the cocksure arrogance of the teen. Upon questioning, they found out he was from a suburb of Chicago and was selling crack cocaine. In Springfield, an ounce of crack that sells for $1,000 in Chicago will sell for as much as $8,000.

Herron admitted to being a member of the Gangster Disciples street gang. His weapon was for the protection of his money and his investment. The police later arrested more than thirty-two people from the Chicago area who also claimed to be members of the Gangster Disciples.

When Herron came into town, things started to change. Violence soon follows gangs and drugs. Tom Snow of the U.S. Marshal Service was part of the Herron investigation. "We started having drive-by shootings. And we don't have those in little old Springfield." Unfortunately, many "little old" towns across America are having drive-by shootings. Chicago- and Los Angeles-based gangs are the leading exporter of gang members. They view cities like Springfield as easy targets because the police are not as experienced in dealing with gangs, and their lack of competition on the streets means more money.

Herron, by the way, was sentenced to thirty-five years in jail. At eighteen years old, the soonest he'll be eligible for release is age forty-nine. That's the way it goes. Prison or the graveyard!

ROBERT SANDIFER

Eleven-year-old Robert Sandifer was nicknamed "Yummy" because of his love for cookies and candy bars, but there was nothing sweet about this kid.

Robert was the third of Lorina Sandifer's seven kids. She had a history of drug abuse and at least thirty misdemeanor arrests. Robert's father went to prison in Wisconsin for drug-related crimes. Robert was beaten and abused as a child and, along with several siblings, became a ward of the court. He was shuttled between foster homes and justice facilities. Eventually, legal guardianship was awarded to his grandmother, Janie Fields, then in her mid-thirties. She was overwhelmed, and the seven kids were soon running wild.

Robert stopped attending school when he was eight years old and spent his time roaming neighborhood streets. It didn't take long for the gangs to latch onto him. Robert became a member of the Black Disciples and kept going downhill from there. He was arrested for shoplifting at age ten, for property damage and armed robbery at eleven, among other crimes.

On an evening in August, he began his final spree. First, he shot Kianta Britten, whom he assumed belonged to a rival gang. Britten survived but was left in a state of partial paralysis. Two hours later, Robert walked out of a dark alley with a semiautomatic weapon in his hands. He sprayed bullets into a crowd of teenagers and killed fourteen-year-old Shavon Dean. His intended target was a rival gang member. Shavon was an innocent person who was in the wrong place at the wrong time.

An intense three-day police search followed. Robert was given refuge by the Black Disciples but they soon began to feel the heat of harboring a wanted killer. Robert became a problem that needed to be eliminated. In the world of assassins, they would call on the "cleaner" to do the job. Cragg Hardaway, aged sixteen, got the assignment. He was picked by older gang generals who send teenagers out into the killing fields. They shift the risk of capture to these kids and assume if they do get caught, they'll be tried as a juvenile and not as an adult. If they're tried as an adult, the leaders don't care anyway.

So Cragg made his move and brought his fourteen-year-old brother along for the ride. They picked up Robert and drove several blocks on that hot August night. According to the younger Hardaway, Cragg then got out of the car and took Robert into a railroad underpass. The brother said he heard three shots fired. Moments later Cragg emerged and said, "It's done."

Shortly after midnight, Robert was found. His head lay in a pool of blood, dirt, and glass; his body was surrounded by gang slogans emblazoned on the walls of the viaduct.

Cragg Hardaway and his brother were charged with murder. There are no winners here. In any gang violence, nobody wins. What are the results of Robert's life? One young girl is dead, another is in a wheelchair, two gang members are in prison for life, and another is in the graveyard.

Unfortunately, Robert's story is not an isolated incident. Cook County Public Guardian Patrick Murphy said, "We see this a hundred times a week." The future is not bright. In fact, criminologists are extremely nervous and they are not the only ones.

Helping Kids Today

Today there are 39 million children under the age of ten in the United States. Many of these kids are growing up in abusive or broken homes with little adult supervision. They lack positive role models and have little direction.

Millions of these children are in danger of becoming "throwaways." According to the American Public Welfare Association, the number of foster children increased from 280,000 in 1986 to 445,000 by June 1993. That's a 59 percent increase and the situation seems to be getting worse.

According to Northeastern University criminologist James Alan Fox, many of these kids are destined to become "temporary sociopaths—impulsive and immature." Easy access to guns and drugs makes them ticking time bombs. Nearly all of the factors that contribute to the rapid increase in youth crime over the past decade are increasing: single-parent households, abuse and neglect, drugs, and inadequate schooling.

Despite the dire forecasts, there are things we can do to turn this around. But this effort begins in the home and must carry over into the schools. Curricula need to be changed to include ways kids can deal with conflict by developing non-aggressive attitudes and behaviors. This involves teaching kids how to resolve conflict without violence, instilling respect in themselves and others, and showing kids how to deal with anger constructively.

Preventing Drug Abuse

Drug abuse thrives everywhere. An estimated 12.5 million Americans now use illegal drugs, according to the U. S. Department of Health and Human Services. Among adults, 74 percent of the drug users were employed. Among young people, a 1995 survey revealed that 48 percent of high school seniors said they'd tried an illegal drug. In another survey, 32 percent of teens said drugs were the most important problem they faced—above violence, sex issues, and getting into college.

Statistics on drug use and abuse tell only part of the story. Many families are left grieving, angry, and desperate for answers. We need stricter laws, public support of police in the enforcement of those laws, education, and family and community leadership.

"We must send a clear message to all Americans: Drugs are illegal, dangerous, unhealthy, and wrong," says the Secretary of Health and Human Services.

The best place to begin is in the home. If parents abuse alcohol or other drugs, legal or illegal, don't be surprised if kids mirror that behavior. Get your own house in order first to provide your kids with positive role models. An important part of this is spending time with your kids. Become involved in their lives, talk to them, meet their friends, and really listen to them, to their ideas, their problems, and their concerns.

You may not agree with them all the time, but that's okay too. You didn't agree with your parents and they didn't agree with theirs. That's the cycle of life and it's not going to change. Why is this important? You may be surprised to realize the prime determinant of drinking or drug use is how many hours the child is left alone during the week.

In single-parent families, or dual-income families, it's not easy to find the time to spend with your kids. But there is nothing more important you can do, so make it a priority. Even a few minutes spent with your children shows you care and that you are interested in their lives. And if you suspect trouble with drugs, don't ignore it. Learn to recognize the symptoms of drug abuse.

First, drug abuse will often produce physical changes in your child. These include sleeplessness, loss of appetite, sudden weight loss, and sustained periods of inactivity followed by sudden bursts of activity.

In many cases, emotional and personality changes occur in tandem with the physical changes. This may include temper tantrums that border on the violent, excessive mood swings, sudden loss of interest in old friends and activities that have always been important to the child, poor grades, and lack of interest in extracurricular activities.

In younger children, I like to compare the effects of drugs to wearing a headset and turning the music up loud. If that child is in a room with other kids and there's a conversation going on, the child's not going to hear it. It's called impairment. This limits the ability of the child to make good choices because he or she may not know what a good choice is.

When it comes to gangs and drugs, parents need to recognize why kids get involved in the first place. Remember the three reasons why kids join the gangs? Peer pressure, intimidation, protection! The best way to beat that is with support and guidance and personal involvement.

If gangs try to recruit your child, he'll talk to you about it. And what should the kids do? When a gang member says, "Declare," to your kid, meaning tell me what gang you've affiliated with, your kid should tell the truth. No lies! No false flagging. Just straight up and honest, "I'm not about gangs, man," or "I play football, I don't have time for that." And then the kid should get out of there.

If a kid is involved in sports or other extracurricular activities, they won't have the time to be involved with gangs. A gang wants the members to give all their attention and loyalty to the gang. Kids who are involved in their families and their communities, sports, church, and have a social life do not have the time to give to the gangs. Keeping your children occupied will limit their vulnerability to gangs.

The same principles apply to the use of drugs. It's about supporting and guiding your child. And how do you do that? Build a bridge of communication with your kids. No topic should be taboo. And do this at a very young age. You cannot build a bridge across a canyon and stress it at the same time. The same with the communication bridge. You build it gradually. Once it's built and you have established an open and honest relationship with your kids, then this bridge will deal with the stress. And that stress might be gangs, drugs, sex, or any number of the tough but essential choices kids are forced to make as they grow up. It's not easy making these choices sometimes. If you have an open relationship, you're in a position to help. Because the kids will come to you if they have a question or have made a mistake.

Guidance About Guns

There are approximately 100 million households in America and nearly half of them contain firearms. In a single year, over 500 children die playing with these weapons. Children and handguns don't mix.

Most parents who own handguns are responsible and cautious. Yet children see and hear more than you think. They love to explore. They can get into places you'd swear were impossible. And many kids are fascinated by guns. They see shootouts on television and they look exciting. Well, they're not. They're deadly.

There are approximately 100 million households in America and nearly half of them contain firearms.

Do you own a handgun? If you don't, chances are high that your neighbor does. And that can mean trouble. Big trouble. Because most children don't know what to do if they find a gun. Do yours?

Like so many of the challenging issues facing parents and kids, this one begins with education. Sit down with your children. Explain to them that shootings on television and in movies are make-believe. In real life, guns kill people. They don't get up after the commercial. Dead is dead!

Assume that your children will encounter a gun. You may not want to think about that but it's a very real possibility. And what should they do? There are three easy steps: Stop; Don't Touch; Run and Tell an Adult. Teach your kids to treat every gun as though it is real and loaded. Many pistols look like toys. In fact, many can be smaller than toys. If your child is playing at someone else's house and he sees a gun, the child should be told to leave the house immediately. There is no reason for the child and the gun to be in the same place.

If you own a gun, it's your responsibility to make sure that no child can ever get hold of it. You can't keep it under your pillow, under the bed, or in an unlocked drawer. Those are the first places that kids—and burglars—look.

Take a firearms course to understand safe handling and storage. Sporting and hunting firearms should be unloaded and securely locked away, with the ammunition locked away in a separate place. There's no reason to keep a hunting rifle loaded.

I'd like to say the same thing for handguns. But, practically speaking, handguns are a different story. Most people with handguns in the home have them for protection. If someone is breaking down your back door and you choose to confront this guy with a weapon, you want that gun to be accessible and loaded. Since loaded guns and kids can be a very dangerous combination, what's the answer? A childproof trigger lock is one way to go. It's a device that prevents the gun from being fired while the lock is on. Another device is the Gun Vault. This is a strong metal container that holds the gun inside. It has a touch pad on the outside that allows for quick access to the gun. This is done by simply sliding the fingers into the slots and releasing the lock with a simple combination of finger presses. These devices will not stop a burglar from taking your gun, but they will, if used properly, keep the small children from killing one another.

Many states have passed laws requiring that guns be locked away, out of the reach of children. I agree. Gun owners should be held fully responsible for securing their weapons. But laws will never substitute for common sense and education. Make sure your home has a heavy dose of both.

Latchkey Kids

By some estimates, as many as 18 million kids are latchkey kids. The children get home from school two or three hours before parents are home from work. On weekends, it might be more than just a couple of hours that children are left alone. It might be most of the day.

Children should be taught to be aware of their actions and surroundings. Teach them to stay in groups and take safe and specified routes to and from school or wherever else they go. When they get near the house, don't dangle house keys in their hand or toss them in the air. Take the keys out of the backpack, open the door immediately, get inside, and lock the door. Don't stay on the doorstep and chat with their friends.

Make sure you have an answering machine and teach your child to screen all calls. If the child doesn't know the caller, they shouldn't pick up the phone. If the child does answer the phone for some reason, they should never acknowledge that they are home alone. If someone asks for a parent, the child should say the parent is busy and take a message.

What happens if a stranger appears at the door? The child should not open the door. If the person at the door persists, or the child senses danger, he or she should call 911 immediately. If the door is opened to a stranger by mistake, the child should not acknowledge that they are alone. Use the same deal as with the phone, say the parent is busy.

If you have a home security system, make sure your child knows how to activate, deactivate, and work the system. This includes the panic button.

The safety of our children is the issue that is the closest to my heart. This quote by Erik H. Erikson sums up my feelings: "Someday maybe there will exist a well-informed, well-considered, and yet fervent public conviction that the most deadly of all possible sins is the mutilation of a child's spirit."

Wouldn't it be great if our society did not tolerate murder, molestation, and abduction of our youth? We can change that by teaching our children to be smart, tough, and aware.

In an interview, I told ABC reporter Chris Wallace that working in murders and rapes for a long time builds up a thick callus but there are certain crimes that go right through all that. If you put your hand on the body of a dead child and still feel the warmth from the body, there is no callus in the world that's going to keep that out of you. That penetrates! We must do whatever it takes to keep our children safe.

Chapter 8
STAYING SAFE ON CAMPUS

Colleges and universities were once considered immune from the violence that has become so much a part of our lives. Author Michael Clay Smith characterized these institutions as "sedate ivory towers, sanctuaries apart from the larger society, and places where crime and criminal justice do not intrude." Today, Smith would undoubtedly write something very different.

This chapter provides information for students going to colleges and universities. It also furnishes the facts and insights necessary for the student and the parents to make informed decisions regarding the safety and security of the student in the dorms, on the quad, in the halls, or while attending activities and parties.

Most young people feel invincible and are probably not too concerned with the issue of campus security when choosing a school. But the safety of the student is very high on the priority scale for most parents.

To get a proper perspective about campus crime, it is important to understand today's college and university campus communities. They are unique. First, the population is primarily eighteen- to twenty-two-year-olds, mostly single, experiencing freedom from home and parental control for the first time.

Another characteristic, especially of residential campuses, is the abundant variety of social activities: parties, athletic events, and fraternity and sorority functions. These events can be breeding grounds for misconduct, indiscretions, misuse of alcohol, and even criminal activity.

The open campus concept can foster criminal activity. Most campuses are barely distinguished from the surrounding community, with no gates, no curfews, and few restrictions on students.

JEANNE ANN CLERY

In April 1986, Jeanne Ann Clery was found dead in her dorm room at Lehigh University. She had been murdered by a fellow student. It was a grisly crime. She was raped, sodomized, beaten, strangled with a metal coil, and mutilated with a broken bottle during the attack.

Her killer, Joseph M. Henry, was soon apprehended after bragging to friends about the murder. The noose further tightened around his neck when police found some of Jeanne's property in his possession. Henry lived off campus but there was no mystery about how he managed to enter the girls' dorm. Students had propped three different doors open with pizza boxes. Each of these doors was equipped with an automatic lock. The students, while making things convenient for themselves, also made it convenient for Henry, who had been on an all-night drinking binge after losing a student election. He turned his drunken rage on Jeanne.

A year after the murder, Henry was found guilty after just two hours and fifteen minutes of jury deliberation. He was sentenced to death in the electric chair. Naturally, he appealed.

The parents of his victim have struggled to deal with the tragedy. The last time they saw their daughter was five days before her death. Mrs. Clery summed up her feelings with these words: "Most Americans saw the space shuttle Challenger splinter into a billion pieces. That's what happened to our hearts."

At the trial, the Clerys learned of security lapses at Lehigh University and, shortly after the verdict was announced, they filed a $25 million suit against the college for negligence. The effects were far-reaching, touching state legislatures, colleges, and concerned parents and students across the country. The Clerys' loss ignited a cause.

The suit was settled out of court but that was only the beginning of the story. They used the settlement, along with their own funds, to launch Security on Campus Inc., a nonprofit clearinghouse for information and advice. They then began lobbying state lawmakers for statutes requiring colleges to publicize their crime statistics. Obviously, this information is never mentioned in splashy, four-color recruiting brochures. Crime on campus is bad for business.

When the Clery family was looking at colleges, safety was a priority. Jeanne's two older brothers had attended Tulane University in New Orleans. Ironically, because of a growing crime problem in that city and the highly publicized murder of a Tulane coed off campus, they decided to look elsewhere.

They picked Lehigh University, located in the gentle rolling hills of Bethlehem, Pennsylvania, about sixty miles from their home. The Clerys and their daughter fell in love with the place. The people were friendly and the campus beautiful. They assumed it was as safe as it looked. What they didn't know was that Lehigh had only twelve security guards to watch over its 5,400 students. They also didn't know that thirty-eight violent crimes—including rape, robbery, and assault—had taken place in the previous three-year period. The University of Pennsylvania, with six times as many students, had just twenty-four violent crimes in that same period.

After Jeanne's tragic death, the Clerys cause fell on very receptive ears. The result? In May 1988, Pennsylvania Governor Robert Casey signed the first bill mandating that all state colleges and universities publish three-year campus-crime reports. In 1990, thanks to the extraordinary efforts of the Clerys and others, the federal Student Right-to-Know and Campus Security Act was passed. It mandates that all colleges and universities whose students receive federal financial aid would be required to issue detailed annual statistics on reported campus crime.

In 1992, an addendum to the act, the Campus Sexual Assault Victims' Bill of Rights, requires colleges and universities to develop programs aimed specifically at reducing sexual assault.

The data provide students and parents with information on serious crime although, like all statistics, they don't tell the whole story. For example, the data are not adjusted for such factors as campus location and size, rendering school-to-school comparisons nearly meaningless. And some schools simply do a better job of reporting crimes.

Six years after passage of the Campus Security Act, the problem of under-reporting violent crime on campus is still widespread. One problem is that Congress gave the Department of Education much of the enforcement power under the 1990 act. David Longenecker, assistant secretary for higher education, told the *New York Times* in early 1996 that the Campus Security Act simply wasn't a priority in his office. "We have limited resources," he said.

A bipartisan bill, HR 2416, drawn up by thirteen House of Representatives members, would require that statistics on crimes on campus—or against students off campus—must be kept in a daily log, written in a form that can be easily understood. The Open Campus Police Logs Act, as it is called, must be open for public inspection.

DANA FOLEY

Dana was living in an apartment complex, directly behind the sorority houses at the University of Georgia, when a man broke into the apartment through a sliding-glass door. She awoke with a pillow over her face.

At first, Dana thought her roommates were fooling around, playing a joke on her. But when she couldn't breathe and the pressure continued, she realized that this was no joke. Dana fought free of the pillow and then felt a punch in the chest. But it was no punch; this guy had a knife. The attacker stabbed her repeatedly but Dana was able to fend him off with her hands. She underwent two major heart surgeries to repair the damage.

Following her ordeal, she did some checking and realized that the Student Right-to-Know and Campus Security Act addressed only crimes committed on campus. So Dana started an organization called Safe Campuses Now, manned by student volunteers.

One member, Sandi Turner, explained why she got involved. "About a month before graduation, my best friend was raped and murdered in her off-campus apartment. Her death was not reported in the University of Georgia's crime statistics. And what's important about that is that she lived closer to the library and academic buildings than most dorms on this campus are."

The University of Georgia is certainly not unique in that regard. Most schools have off-campus housing in and around the immediate vicinity of the institution. So if you, or someone close to you, plans to live off campus, I suggest you check out the crime statistics. If the school doesn't know, find out why. Then find out where to get the information you seek.

Campus Security Checklist

When it comes to selecting a college or university, there are any number of factors to consider. The issue of safety is one I suggest you include as part of your evaluation. The following checklist will help you in your evaluation.

√ You can begin by getting a copy of the federal crime report from the admissions office. By law, any prospective student is entitled to receive a copy. This report will include statistics on crimes for the past three years, as well as a description of campus security policies. The thoroughness of the report and straightforward language will tell you a lot about the college's approach.

√ To really get the lay of the land, you need to visit the campus. Do it when classes are in session. Otherwise the campus might look like a ghost town. When classes are in session, there is activity day and night, so it's a good idea to tour the facilities at both of these times. Check out academic buildings, residence halls, and other facilities. Are walkways, quadrangles, parking lots, and park areas well lit?

√ Are there uniformed campus police? Are they a real presence or invisible? What is their relationship to local law enforcement agencies? This is especially important since many students live off campus, creating some unique challenges.

√ Incidents of crime and misconduct often result in "town vs. gown" tensions that require the cooperation, communication, and mutual assistance of both departments to respond effectively. Some towns resent the onslaught of students every September even though the students may be bringing in a lot of revenue. Also, check out the areas surrounding the campus. Do neighborhoods appear safe, with well-lit streets, an absence of graffiti? Because if there is graffiti, there are most likely gangs.

And if there are gangs nearby there will be drugs and violence. If that's the case, you might want to drop that school from your consideration. Of course some of our most prestigious institutions of higher learning are located in urban areas, many surrounded by marginal to bad neighborhoods. That's not a reason to dismiss them outright. It is a reason to be especially thorough in your security check.

√ Are commuter buses on regular schedules? Are bus stops well lit? Are there emergency telephones located throughout the campus with direct links to the campus security office?

√ Check out the campus, fraternity row, and student hangouts on a Saturday night. Certain schools become labeled—by the students, certainly not the administration—as being party schools. And with parties comes alcohol. And when alcohol use becomes abused, it's a problem on campus like anywhere else. By being observant, you can determine whether the students are simply partying and having a good time or if they are out of control.

Why is this important? Because alcohol is involved in as many as ninety percent of violent crimes on campus. Often, this includes both the offender and the victim, especially in cases of sexual assault.

In any case, don't be afraid to ask questions. The admissions counselor can direct you to the proper source to best answer those questions from the administration's perspective. It's also good to check with residence hall advisors and other students. You'll get the straight scoop from them. They won't pull any punches.

What to Ask

• What are the most common crimes? Since vandalism and theft top the list at most schools, dig deeper. Find out about crimes that may be of particular concern to

---

you, such as muggings, sexual harassment, and date rape. If your son or daughter is planning to pledge a fraternity or sorority, check out any incidences of hazing.

- What specific steps does the school take to combat crime? Emergency outdoor phones, well-lit buildings and walkways, uniformed guards are certainly part of the mix. But what else?
- How involved are students? At UCLA, for example, 300 community service officers—all students who have received special training from the university police department—patrol the campus, act as escorts for other students at night (remember, safety in numbers), and assist the police by taking minor crime reports.
- How does the school's judicial system work? Most schools have administrator/faculty/student tribunals which deal with minor offenses such as vandalism and alcohol violations. Sometimes this forum may address more serious violations such as date rape when the victim is reluctant to press charges or the prosecutors feel they lack evidence for a conviction.

  The Dean of Students can usually provide you with information on the consistency and effectiveness of the system in dealing with problem students.

- Does the school provide medical, psychological, and legal help to victims of crime on campus? Are there rape crisis counselors available? Are serious crimes dealt with head-on? When a serious crime does occur, is the student newspaper and radio station informed? This is to alert students to potential danger and encourage witnesses to come forward. It will also ensure there is no cover-up by the administration.
- Is the school active in educational programs designed to curb alcohol abuse? Is drinking and driving actively discouraged, with alternatives available such as a designated driver program?
- Does the institution conduct regular and consistent crime prevention programs? I have personally appeared at countless colleges and universities to deliver my Tough Target presentation.

The same rules apply on campus as they do any other place. The Tough Target does not get picked. Simply keeping doors locked whenever they leave their dorm rooms and apartments—and when sleeping—can help students avoid a lot of trouble. Since about eighty percent of all campus crime is committed by other students, valuable jewelry, stereo equipment, and expensive bikes should be left at home.

As noted earlier, the abuse of illegal drugs and alcohol is a major contributor to crime on campus. According to the *Chronicle of Higher Education*, drug arrests on college campuses increased twenty-three percent in 1994 over 1993. Alcohol-related offenses were up 5.6 percent during that same period. Students need to use common sense when it comes to drinking and other activities.

To their credit, Lehigh University administrators did not try to downplay the Clery tragedy. Instead, they took action. They increased the security force by 25 percent, implemented twenty-four-hour-a-day patrols in residence halls, added a new emergency phone system, and an evening shuttle service. Speaking out does help to prevent crime!

JACKSONVILLE STATE UNIVERSITY

Jacksonville State University (JSU), in Alabama, is another good example of a school that tackled this issue head-on. Responding to a rise in campus crime, JSU conducted a careful analysis that indicated 65 percent of the criminal incidents occurring on campus took place in and around residence halls. Not surprisingly, they found that special events such as concerts and sporting events contributed significantly.

In addition to the analysis, campus police administrators also carefully reviewed the efforts implemented by several other universities in dealing with similar problems. Based on this analysis and research, JSU administrators developed strategies to address the problem of crime and violence via a community-based crime prevention program.

At the outset, the university's police department enhanced the existing nighttime security escort service for female students and implemented a residence hall foot patrol. The department also used a bike patrol to increase its crime prevention efforts and to establish better public relations with students.

Importantly, other campus groups were recruited to help make the campus safer. Counselors and health care personnel assisted campus police officers in dramatically increasing the number of crime prevention presentations to students. Students became more involved in security issues related to housing, special events, and cultural diversity programs. A coordinated effort was implemented to ensure that the campus judicial system dealt promptly and firmly with students who presented a threat to campus safety.

A program to heighten awareness of alcohol abuse was implemented and increased enforcement of alcohol violations. The university's police department also worked closely with local police to deal with neighborhood complaints. The two agencies established a mutual reporting and first-responder procedure for off-campus fraternity disturbances.

And finally, underlying the entire effort was the adoption of a zero-tolerance philosophy toward weapons violations and violent behavior. Campus police, university officials, and local law enforcement worked together to create a threat-free environment.

Jacksonville State University's strategy is solid and successful. If the colleges or universities your family is considering do not take an aggressive stance toward crime—and the honest reporting of it—you might want to look elsewhere.

When my own children were picking their colleges and doing campus tours, I visited the local police departments. I asked them about the crime around campus. I asked them about drugs and alcohol-related crimes in the area. I did this because there is a blurring of boundaries between the campus and the community.

Unlike a college, which has something to lose and may encourage students not to report crime, the local police department has no vested interest in the college and will tell you the truth. When a crime is committed on campus it is reported to the campus police and they must make it part of their annual report. If a crime occurs across the street from the campus boundary, then it does not have to be included in the report. Local city police have copies of the reports from the campus as well as information on the city crime.

Don't narrow your focus to just the campus. Students cross paths and interact with the townspeople every day. They live in the community as well as at the university. A visit to the city police will give you a real picture of the crime.

Alcohol and Crime

Alcohol is an all too common denominator in many incidents of campus crime. When it comes to rape and sexual assault, as many as 50 percent of victims and 75 percent of their attackers were, or had been, drinking.

And here's something every person who thinks of "loosening up" a woman with alcohol would be wise to take to heart: The legal definition of rape turns on the notion of consent. Taking advantage of any woman too drunk to be capable of giving that consent is rape. Abuse of alcohol means giving up control. This has nothing to do with who is right or wrong when a crime comes down, or guilt or innocence. It's just the way it is. Drinking to excess can mean a lot more than a bad hangover.

A study sponsored by the Association of American Colleges Project indicates that members of closely knit, all-male groups such as fraternities and athletic teams are involved in a disproportionate number of rapes, especially those committed by a group. They can be encouraged to prove their sexual prowess to the other members of the group. This results in these guys participating in a group rape when they might never commit rape alone.

MARY JONES

Mary was a freshman, wanting to fit in. She was invited by twenty-three-year-old Daniel Ortarsh to a party at the prestigious Pi Kappa Alpha fraternity house. A little tequila, she thought, would help ease her nervousness. A lot would set her free.

When she arrived at the frat house, her date handed her a bottle of wine and left her in his room to finish it off. Tests would later place her blood-alcohol level at .349 percent, which can cause death.

Mary has no recollection of what happened next. Police reports say that Ortarsh had sex with her, then moved her to the shower room, where he was joined by at least two other fraternity brothers for more sex. She was later found next door, where she had been dumped unconscious with her skirt up, her panties down, and the initials of another fraternity scrawled in ballpoint pen on her thighs. One of the boys admitted to the rape, the rest denied it.

Over the next several months, she was the subject of intense scrutiny from other students and defense lawyers for the alleged rapists. It nearly drove her crazy. She was filled with shame. Mary left school, and eventually checked into a psychiatric hospital near her home. "There, I just lost interest in the quality of my life," she said. Suffering from alcoholism, bulimia, and depression, she tried to commit suicide.

Two of Ortarsh's fraternity brothers plea-bargained to lesser charges prior to his trial. He pleaded no contest. By this time, Mary had begun to recover. The judge prevented the defense from inquiring into Mary's sexual history as part of the discovery process. This was a first for a rape case in Florida.

The judge gave Ortarsh a sentence of a year minus a day, considered severe for a date-rape case. A police officer saw this ruling as a milestone. "Years ago, probably months ago, the opinion would have been that Mary drank of her own accord and was responsible for what happened. This makes people aware that what happened to her is rape."

Years later, Mary, like virtually all rape victims, can't forget or forgive. Mary is in no way responsible for the actions of the fraternity brothers, but a woman is in a much better position to deal with her environment and potentially dangerous situations if she is in control. Mary wasn't. She was not only drunk—she drank herself into unconsciousness.

SARAH MILLER

Alcohol was also involved in the case of Sarah Miller but it did not appear to be the primary motivator.

Sarah Miller was left bruised and bleeding in her dormitory room on the campus of Lake Superior State University in Michigan. Sarah had attended a party with David Caballero, a member of the university's varsity wrestling squad, and he escorted her back to her room. There, he forced her to have intercourse with him and to perform oral sex.

Sarah reported the crime and Caballero was arrested and brought to trial. In court, he was nonchalant, testifying that the victim had consented to have sex with him and then complained because he was overzealous. He told the court, "It was just your average one-night stand or whatever." Judge Stark saw it differently and said, "I see a young man who believed that 'if it's my word against hers, nothing can happen.' You did not have consent and you knew you didn't have consent."

Despite his position, Stark set aside a verdict of first-degree criminal sexual conduct and, instead, gave Caballero three years probation and assessed some modest fines. Stark later told the press that a felony conviction would have been too harsh because it would ruin any chance for the defendant to realize his dream of becoming a police officer. Unfortunately, verdicts like this send a loud and clear message that you can sexually assault someone and get off with a slap on the wrist. That's got to change. And so does educating young people. They need to know where to draw the line.

An excellent example of a proactive approach is that taken by George Mason University. The school publishes a brochure entitled "Sexual Assault: One in Four." The brochure refers to research that reports one in four women college students are victims of rape or attempted rape. This brochure clearly states the university's no-tolerance stance against any sexual offenses, how to reduce the risks, what to do if victimized by sexual assault, and the consequences for those who commit sexual assault.

Chapter 9

SAFETY-CONSCIOUS SENIORS

The American Association of Retired People (AARP) reports current membership of older Americans in excess of 33 million people and the senior population is growing. Today, one in eight Americans is over sixty-five and by the year 2025, the number of Americans over sixty-five will outnumber teenagers by more than two to one. More than 9 million seniors live by themselves.

When people refer to this segment of the population they use chronological age as the defining factor—equivalent to going out to pasture. But times are changing.

The recent crop entering their golden years are a whole new breed. They tend to be more active and involved. Generally speaking, they are healthier and wealthier than those who preceded them. For many, their psychological and physical age defies their chronological age. They think, act, look, and feel much younger than they are.

On the other end of the spectrum are those whose health, both physically and mentally, is failing rapidly, leaving them disabled or infirm.

In the middle—the vast majority of older Americans—are those who enjoy good health, both physically and psychologically, but cannot escape the inevitable march of time. This makes them less able to defend themselves if attacked, less able to escape trouble, slower to bounce back from injury, and easier targets for cons and scams.

What we typically refer to as seniors or the elderly is a very diverse group. The advice on personal safety in this chapter can be useful to anyone but it is targeted primarily to the majority of older men and women who are still active both physically and mentally.

Paralyzing Fear

Justice Department research indicates that, in comparison to their younger counterparts, older Americans are more sensitive to the issues of crime and personal security, and have a much deeper fear of the physical and emotional trauma associated with crime.

This fear promotes feelings of isolation and helplessness, and leaves many elderly citizens increasingly vulnerable to mental depression, illness, and crime.

For many older Americans, even a minor crime such as a purse snatching can cause major emotional, physical, and financial trauma. The best antidote to this fear is knowledge about:

• the reality of crime rates

• avoiding victimization

• how to respond when crime strikes

If our seniors were armed with this information, they'd be better prepared to retain control over their lives, remain independent, and feel self-sufficient. It's peace of mind for them and their children.

Overcoming "Camp Mentality"

"Camp Mentality" is a term used to describe those who try to escape crime by staying inside. People with this fear lock their doors and windows and often lose the social contacts necessary to maintain good mental health. This is also detrimental to their physical well-being since it limits their ability to get out and walk.

Case in point:

In the summer of 1995, an oppressive heat wave hit the city of Chicago, killing over 600 people. Many were elderly citizens without air conditioning but they remained locked inside their homes with the windows locked because they were afraid of being victims of crime.

Camp Mentality describes those who try to escape crime on the outside by staying inside.

The way to alleviate this fear is by teaching seniors the Tough Target strategy. Crimes of opportunity are the most common forms of crime against the elderly. Among the most popular crimes of opportunity are home burglaries, muggings, and purse snatchings.

MARGARET WILKINSON

Robbery is the crime that sixty-four-year-old Margaret Wilkinson faced. In a letter she describes her frightening experience:

Dear Mr. Bittenbinder:

I am writing you to thank you for teaching me to be a Tough Target. I honestly believe that you either saved my life or you saved me from harm.

On December 10, 1994, I was at a company Christmas party. Because parking was limited, I ended up parking about three blocks away. I picked a well-lit city parking lot and joined the crowds that were walking towards the lot. I decided to leave my purse in the trunk for safety reasons.

I left the party early, about 10:30 P.M. My car was the only one left in the parking lot and as I approached it, two scary-looking men came towards me. One was in a wheelchair, the other was pushing it. I sensed that these guys were up to no good.

One of the gifts from the party was a Santa mug. I held it in my hand when the tall one came at me. I started swinging the cup at him. All the while I was screaming and yelling for him to get away. He stopped in his tracks. He seemed surprised and unprepared.

Because my car has a code that unlocks the doors, I had a key hidden under the seat. I got in the car, started it, put it in reverse, and I didn't look back. They kept screaming that I was a crazy lady and that he wanted to ask me for directions. I'm glad that I didn't let my guard down and become another statistic.

This is a success story because this woman who was not afraid to trust her instincts got away safely. Margaret's safety is the most important part of this story. She did some things wrong and some things right but she had a "whatever it takes" attitude and managed to get away.

- When these two strange men approached, she acted immediately and decisively. Were these guys really legit and just looking for directions? Maybe, maybe not. It doesn't matter. Margaret is safe and that's all that counts. If Margaret were wrong and these two guys really did need directions, what's the damage? None. They just think that she's a crazy lady and they'll want to get away from her. If they were not legit and she thinks, "Oh, I better be nice and polite and help these men," her purse might not have been the only thing locked in that trunk. It might have been her body. So put yourself in her position. What would you do? Make that decision now, not in the heat of battle.

- She parked in a well-lit city lot. That was smart. But when it gets late, those lots empty out. So she should have asked someone at the party to escort her to her car. That's the safest way to go.

- Margaret used her resources to protect herself. She used the only thing she had in hand—a Santa mug. Her Santa mug was certainly not as good as pepper spray but it's all she had and it bought her enough time to get into her car.

- Hiding a spare key under the seat was not a good idea because that's where car thieves look. I recommend that you carry your car keys in hand with pepper spray attached.

- Yelling and screaming caught these guys off guard and that was also smart. She locked the doors immediately and got out of there. She didn't wait for them to try to smash her window or whatever else they might do. She was gone.

Margaret made some mistakes and there were certainly things she could have done to be a tougher target. But she was tough enough. She survived this incident by having a plan and by taking action.

LOWELLA RIVERO

Lowella Rivero, a sixty-three-year-old secretary, was heading for home on an autumn night. She was on foot and had just turned onto the block where she lived when she sensed she was being followed. She turned around, didn't see anyone, and didn't worry too much about it. She was close to home and felt safe in her own neighborhood.

Suddenly, without warning, she was attacked. The guy jumped her from behind, knocking her down to the ground. It was clear he wanted more than her purse. So Lowella swiveled around on her backside and kicked and screamed for all she was worth. After a short struggle and a few good shots to the shins and knees, the bad guy ran off. He quickly realized that he got more than he bargained for.

Lowella did exactly the right thing in this situation. She used her legs to keep this guy off her, and yelled and screamed at him, which kept her from being raped, or even killed.

Lowella used her legs and Margaret used a Santa cup. In both incidents, Margaret and Lowella used their voices to scream and attract attention. The voice is an especially valuable tool for older people who may not be able to run from the scene.

Taking Preventative Measures

If you have a plan, you can protect yourself before even leaving the house. Follow these tips to keep you safe:

Glasses

If you wear glasses, buy a chain to affix to the glasses. One of the first things an attacker will do is knock the glasses off the face of the older victim. This action dilutes the identification of the offender and disorients the victim. But if you have a chain on the glasses, they'll fall only to your chest and not on the ground, which means they won't be stepped on by either the bad guy or you. I recommend a chain instead of a cord because if he grabs the chain, it should break. If he grabs the cord it will not break and now he has a noose around your neck.

Money

Keep a small amount of cash (for things like quick purchases or cab fares) separate from your purse or wallet. If you're being watched, you won't be revealing how much cash you have on your person (which shouldn't be a lot anyway). If you don't like to use credit cards, carry checks.

When it comes to cash, keep it in the bank where it belongs. There are too many stories of couples who stashed their life savings at home and lose it all in a matter of moments. They may lose it because they were victims of a scam or by simply leaving doors unlocked when they're outside. The majority of burglaries involving older citizens are a result of unlocked doors and windows.

Get involved

You can also work with your bank to have government, pension, or annuity checks deposited directly into your account. Many banks offer this as a free service to older citizens. Then you're not walking around with large amounts of cash or rushing to get to the bank when the weather is bad.

Get involved in a neighborhood watch program and attend the meetings. You will meet your neighbors in a common cause. If you know your neighbors you may be suspicious when strangers are moving their TV and stereo into a van and you can call the police to check out the situation.

This neighborhood watch idea has no down side. People feel safer outdoors if they feel the people in the other houses are not just unknown residents of the block, but are neighbors in the true sense of the word. Post signs on your block that say "We Call Police" or "Neighborhood Watch." If there are two streets in a residential area and one of the streets is posted with signs that indicate a watch and the other street is not posted, which street do you think the bad guy will target?

Establish daily telephone contact with family or neighbors. If there's trouble—from crime or injury or illness—you will not be isolated for any extended period of time. Consider having a home security system installed. A monitored system with panic buttons can also help protect you from crime and get help in time of illness or injury. Make sure you have extension phones installed on every level of your home for safety and security.

Street smarts

- Women should carry a fanny pack and not a purse. A fanny pack also works well for men. The bad guys don't like fanny packs because they're too much trouble to rip off. If you are wearing one under your jacket or blouse, they cannot see it. If you can keep the bad guy from seeing the target, he won't try for it and you are a tougher target. Plain and simple. Remember to carry a pepper spray on your key ring, or a personal alarm.
- If you are out on the streets and attacked, use that pepper spray. If you carry a cane, use the cane on his groin. Raising the cane over your head to strike a blow is not effective. It is too easy to block. It takes too long to do it and requires more strength. Hold the cane out in front of you with the end pointed toward the ground at a forty-five-degree angle. If you are attacked, swing the cane upwards and strike him in the groin. This blow is harder to block, faster, and takes less strength.
- If you're confronted and all this guy wants is your purse or wallet or coat, give it up. Don't argue and don't plead or beg. The bad guy wants to control the situation and you want it to end. Don't let him have the upper hand psychologically. Throw the money or wallet one way and go the other way.

   If this guy wants to take you into a car or to another location, you've got to fight because it is very likely that it will be a fight for your life.

Be inconspicuous in appearance when you go out. If you are driving, bring your cell phone and know exactly where you are going. Don't take shortcuts into unfamiliar territory, especially at night, when the landmarks may be obscured by lower lighting conditions. This applies to a shopping trip across town or a trip across country.

Report All Incidents

If you are the victim of a crime, report it. Too many crimes against older people go unreported because they fear retribution and they don't want to be hassled filing a report or being required to go to court. Others fear appearing weak and vulnerable to their children.

Some people don't report a crime because they think, "The police won't catch him anyway." Well, the police won't even look for him if they don't know a crime has occurred. Police departments need the help of citizens in order to help everyone.

CASE IN POINT: Three people are robbed on the street by the same offender. In each case the victim was not able to get the license plate number on the getaway car. Victim number one, John, was robbed during the day and he described the car as a a blue two-door with dark windows.

Victim number two, Mary, was robbed at night and she could not tell the color but said that the first part of the license number was ABC. The rest she could not read as the car was speeding off.

Victim number three, Sue, was robbed at dusk. Sue was also unable to get the entire plate number. She did, however, remember that the last part of the plate was 123.

With all this information, the detectives who read these reports and process the information have a description of the car and the entire license plate number. If any of these people had not reported the crime, none of the incidents would be solved and the bad guy would not have been arrested. Each person had a piece of the information and had no idea of the existence of the other parts. You may not have all the information or a complete description, but what you know is important and may be needed to solve other crimes. Report all incidents of crime because you never know whose life you could be saving.

Learn About CAPS

More and more police departments are instituting, promoting, and sponsoring programs where the citizens have direct access to the police. The Chicago Alternative Policing Strategies (CAPS) is such a group. Citizens' groups, individuals, PTAs, and merchant associations are able to make requests and suggestions to the city to make it a safer place. Traffic lights, stop signs, and streetlights are installed at the request of the neighborhood. Trees are trimmed for greater visibility. Abandoned buildings used for drug sales and hangouts for gangs are condemned and destroyed by the building department. These citizens have input.

Their plan works because the changes requested—whether they are for more police coverage, for the use of special undercover teams, for a streetlight in a darkened area of a block—are addressed in a timely manner by the city. Changes are then quickly implemented. This way the residents see the progress and are encouraged to become more involved. When residents become more involved in their community, it is one of the best things that can happen.

In addition to the physical changes to the neighborhoods, the police department can also use the program to ask for help locating criminals. If your community doesn't have such a program, find out why. CAPS works.

Understanding Con Games

Often referred to as cons and scams, confidence games are big business. We hear or read about them every day in the headlines: "Woman, 100, Lost $571,000 in Scam." It's true. It happened to a Chicago woman.

Delta Clampett, also pushing the century mark, was told by a friendly repairman that she needed a new flue for her fireplace. It cost her $800, then another $1,000, and then another $1,100. It nearly wiped her out.

The Top Ten list of scams for the nineties involves loan fees, telemarketing sales of all kinds, home improvements, auto repairs, and employment services. Some of these are new. Some are not. And, of course, the old standbys, such as the Pigeon Drop and the Bank Examiner scam, never go out of style. We'll look at several of these cons and what you need to know to avoid being taken.

What exactly is a confidence game? It's simple. If there is deception involved, it's fraud. And fraud is a crime. A crime that costs billions! Telemarketing fraud alone is estimated by the National Fraud Information Center (NFIC) at over $40 billion a year. The U.S. Office of Consumer Affairs estimates the total fraud business to be $100 billion per year. That's certainly some piece of change!

There are some smart and devious people running con games because this is a different breed of criminal. They are aggressive, persuasive, and smart. And they know how to exploit the credibility of newspapers, television, the Internet, and the U.S. mails.

The con artist contradicts many of the traits of the street criminal. The con artist is aggressive, persuasive, and smart.

The con artist uses weapons much more subtle than a gun or knife. His weapons are a winning smile, a stylish appearance, a sharp tongue, and shrewd methods to gain inside information about your life and your finances.

Remember the victim side of the faulty logic equation? That's where the victim says, "It can't happen to me!" Well, if you think you're too smart or too savvy to be taken by a con, think again. There's a huge club out there whose members felt the same way. It can be very difficult to say no to a con artist.

Con artists do not discriminate. Age, gender, race, income level—it doesn't matter. They go after them all. Many people believe those who fall prey to confidence games are either greedy, gullible, or brain dead. That's not the case. It can happen to anyone.

Cons, like all criminals, go for the easy target. Simply put, many older Americans are easy targets. That's just the way it is. And today, they are at greater risk than ever before. Here are some primary reasons:

• Older people are often better off financially. According to the Bureau of the Census, the median net worth of households headed by a person age sixty-five or over is substantially higher than any other age group.

• They have more leisure time. Longer life spans, better health, earlier retirement, absence of job and family responsibilities often translate into empty hours. As one veteran Bunco cop in Florida said, "The same group of seniors would call over and over again to report a crime or someone suspicious in the neighborhood. We learned over time there was no crime or suspicious person. They just wanted to talk to somebody." To a con man, this is very good news.

• Separation and worry. The retirement communities that flourish in such states as Florida and Arizona offer independence and a chance to meet new friends. But for many, these warm-weather havens mean moving thousands of miles away from families and old friends. An individual feeling a sense of loneliness and isolation is often very receptive to some guy with a warm smile and a hot deal!

- Physical and mental factors. Many older Americans find that their mental faculties may be declining. Perhaps they don't think as clearly as they once did or they become easily confused, perfect for the crafty con man.

Here are some of the most common scams you should know about:

Home Repair Scams

Free inspections that reveal problems, workers who just happen to be in the neighborhood, and bargain-basement prices for what would normally be expensive jobs, have fraud written all over them. Common home repair scams involve driveway paving, roofing repair, termite extermination, tree pruning, and furnace repair.

Often, they quote unusually low prices because they have "leftover materials."

One guy from Indianapolis, Indiana, offers to do home repair jobs at a fraction of the cost of his competitors. He requires an up-front fee of several hundred dollars and then never does the work. He'll occasionally take calls from disgruntled customers but they are rarely successful at getting him to complete the promised work. Instead, he offers one excuse after the other. Many of his victims finally give up or call the police.

Since no permit is required for these small jobs, it's difficult for anyone to prove fraud. So this guy simply thumbs his nose at the law and moves on to the next target, operating under a new company name.

Your best defense against these guys?

- Stop—question—think! Don't sign anything or do anything until you check them out. Ask for references. If this guy is legit, he'll be happy to give you the names of satisfied customers.
- Call the Better Business Bureau. They often know of disreputable operators. Be especially wary of high-pressure tactics, demands for cash only, the need for a quick decision, or secret deals.

ERNEST AND BETTY WINSTON

Ernest and Betty Winston of Clarence, New York, were not lonely or worried but they were trusting. They were relaxing on the front porch of their tidy, two-story frame home one hot morning in August when two men in their thirties came calling. The men were neatly dressed in dark blue work uniforms with their first names printed on the shirts. Both were carrying clipboards. It all seemed innocent enough, but it was a day the Winstons would never forget.

The two men introduced themselves to the Winstons as Bill and Tim from City Water Works. It seemed some neighbors were having problems with their water pressure. Both men were very friendly and professional. They were quick to get started on the so-called problem.

Ernest seemed a little leery of these guys and was thinking out loud about calling the water company. Tim said, "Sure, go ahead. But he's not in the office right now. In fact, he's over in the next block helpin' out some folks there. I'll give you the number and maybe we'll have time to come back later. We'll just go next door for now. I'm sure your neighbor can use the fifty bucks."

Fifty bucks was something Ernest had not heard about earlier. The men explained that fifty dollars was going to be given to all the households because of the inconvenience.

Tim follows Betty to the upstairs bathroom while Bill gives Ernest a one-hundred dollar bill. Bill explained that he didn't have any change so Ernest goes upstairs to get some. In the meantime Tim sends Betty downstairs while he finishes making his estimate. Of course Tim is noticing where Ernest keeps all his cash.

It wasn't until later that morning when Ernest and Betty discovered their loss. A ten thousand dollar loss! And it nearly wiped out their entire savings. The business card, of course, was bogus, like everything else these guys did.

The Winstons trusted these strangers because they seemed "official" and they were nice, friendly guys. You can't do that. Remember, con artists live off their wits and charm. Like these two guys, they will be neatly dressed, talkative, and very convincing. That's how they gain your confidence.

- Don't make the obvious mistake and keep large sums of cash around the house. It's an invitation to trouble. Keep money in the bank where it belongs. If you think the big banks seem cold and impersonal, find a smaller bank. They are all insured by the federal government and your money will be safe.

  They exploit loneliness, greed, or disabilities. In the beginning Mr. Winston was not comfortable with this whole scene, but a quick fifty bucks seemed like a good deal at the time. If a deal or an offer seems too good to be true, it probably is! Ernie should have trusted his instincts and called to check these guys out. That's the thing to do with any utility workers. Looking at a set of credentials isn't enough because phony ID is easy to fabricate.

  If an offer seems too good to be true, it is.

- Don't ever call a number they give you! That could simply connect you to another con artist. Look up the number in the phone book! If they are legit, they'll wait. If not, they'll be out of there and your problem is over. Most of these con artists are not going to be violent. They want cash or property not confrontation.

- Keep in mind these con artists are everywhere. They've got a million stories to tell and they rely on confusion and momentum. Their number one tactic is to keep you from thinking. But you've got to interrupt that momentum and take control of the situation. If you don't understand what they're saying, make them slow down until you are satisfied with their answer and then check out the situation. Ernie and Betty were never given a moment to gather their thoughts. These guys kept them busy the entire time they were there.

  Take the time to stop, to question, and to think.

- These guys want to keep you off guard. That's why most of these con artists work in teams. They will talk you into a corner and make even the craziest proposition seem plausible, like getting fifty bucks from the city just to test the water pressure!

  You may not be involved in a scenario like that but you should learn from it. These guys crafted a very convincing story and Ernest and Betty believed them because they didn't trust their instincts and check it out.

The Friendly Stranger

Always keep the doors locked if you are working outside. It only takes a minute to put that key in your pocket and secure your home. If you don't, you may be the victim of a friendly passerby. He'll distract you with some flattering comment about your yard or garden while his accomplice slips in the open door and robs you blind.

If someone approaches you and wants to use your phone, offer to make the call for them but make them wait outside. Get to know your neighbors and watch out for one another. Be especially careful after a death in the family—these guys will often check obituaries and strike soon after the loss of a spouse.

The Bank Examiner

Another popular scam involves someone posing as a bank official, IRS agent, or law enforcement official. This person will ask for your help in a sting operation to test the honesty of a teller at your bank. You'll be asked to withdraw a sizable sum of money from your account and turn it over to this person so the serial numbers can be checked or the money marked. You may even be offered a reward.

In exchange for the cash, you are given a very official-looking receipt that looks every bit as official as the ID of the person who contacted you. You are then told to go home, sit by the phone, and wait for the call that makes you a hero for helping to nab the dishonest teller.

The call, of course, never comes and the money is gone!

The Pigeon Drop

The story varies, the con doesn't. In one approach, a stranger pulls you aside as you are near your bank and tells you she found a bag containing a large sum of cash. She opens it and, sure enough, when you look inside there's a bundle of green. She claims to be nervous carrying around this much money or she has an urgent appointment and asks you to go to the authorities with it.

In exchange, the woman agrees to split the loot with you if no report of missing money has been filed with the police. And to ensure that you don't run off with the cash, she asks for some "good faith" money. You agree. After all, it could be found money. So you go inside and withdraw the money and hand it over to the woman.

She hands you a slip of paper with a phone number on it and tells you to call her as soon as you know the status of the money. What she doesn't tell you, of course, is that she switched the bags. She goes one way with your cash, you go the other with a bag containing nothing but shredded newspaper inside.

The Pigeon Drop often involves a team approach but the basic con is the same.

The Pyramid Scheme

The traditional pyramid scheme involves payment of a certain sum of money to the name at the top of the list and also a similar amount to the person bringing you into the deal. There's often no product involved. Your goal is to move up to the top of the list to collect money from all those farther down before the pyramid collapses. The scheme can involve a geometric progression that can run into the hundreds of thousands of dollars.

A variation of the pyramid is the Ponzi scheme, named after Carlo Ponzi who swindled fellow immigrants in the early twentieth century. In this scam, the Ponzi artist secures investments in such things as commodities, inventories, managed investment accounts, or phony stocks. The guy then pockets the money in exchange for "paper profit" statements.

If someone does demand a payout, he then "robs Peter to pay Paul" taking new investors' money to make the payoff. Sooner or later, the whole thing collapses. Chances are by the time that happens, the bad guy is at a lavish resort in some far-off place, drinking margaritas and spending your money.

Telemarketing Fraud

Telemarketing is big business. So naturally telemarketing fraud is too. One approach that these guys use is to lure potential victims of phone fraud with newspaper ads, television spots, or direct mail. In these scams, the victim initiates the call. However it comes down, you can be taken big time.

One trick they use is to tell you that you're a sweepstakes finalist and that you have won a fabulous vacation package or big-screen television set but to claim the prize you must provide credit card information.

The second most frequent type of fraud, after the popular sweepstakes scam, is travel fraud. It might involve the receipt of a "vacation certificate" for a free trip. When consumers call to claim their prize, they get buried in a stream of credit card charges to redeem or verify the certificate.

Telemarketing schemes for travel fraud are also popular. You get a phone call proposing a trip at an unheard of price, or a huge discount because of a drop in tourism in a particular area, say Arizona. Of course, you need to provide a credit card number immediately to take advantage of the offer.

Don't fall for it. If winning a prize or a trip involves paying something up front, refuse it. It's a scam. In late 1995, the FBI nabbed over 400 people in fifteen states in a blitz against telemarketing scams that preyed on the elderly. As part of their investigation, they recorded calls from the con artists.

Many of these calls included insults and threats. One elderly woman was told to send $15,000 to claim her $50,000 prize. When she began to cry, the caller attacked her, saying, "I'm trying to give you your money here and you're going to your grave a loser!"

Fraudulent charity organizations, such as the American Cancer Association instead of the American Cancer Society or the Fraternal Brotherhood of Police instead of the Fraternal Order of Police, may call and ask for cash donations or your credit card number—don't give it to them.

Never give your credit card or calling card number to someone who calls you and asks for it. I know one story where a man was awakened at three A.M. by a call from a man claiming to be with the Federal Communications Commission (FCC). The caller asked if any calls had been made to Japan earlier that evening. Still shaking off the effects of sleep, he said no. The caller then told him they had traced over $700 worth of calls to his number in the last several hours and he was calling to help.

Now, the guy who made the call was friendly and articulate and very official sounding. Naturally, there was concern. Then Mr. FCC asked for his calling card number. It was then that the man got suspicious. He refused and that was that. The other guy hung up and tried to scam someone who was not as sharp.

A pretty slick little con. Another way these guys will try to steal phone card numbers is by lurking about airports and other public places. They will pretend to be talking on the next pay phone and making notes. What they are really doing is writing down the phone card numbers of the unsuspecting victims at the next phone stall. Many of these victims are in a hurry and have no idea they've been had.

Mail Fraud

A federal law protects consumers from fraud via the mails. However, not all misleading advertising is fraudulent. Many mail order con artists don't necessarily lie but they stretch the truth to the limits. Some examples: One goof offered a "Hide-A-Swat" product guaranteed to kill flies and pests for only $9.95. It was a rolled-up newspaper.

Another hot offer was a "Universal Coat Hanger" for only $3.99. Those who ordered this marvel really got nailed. Literally. They were sent a nail!

You get the picture. So watch out for these scams that skirt the law but still rip you off. Mail swindlers often use official-looking forms and slick advertising approaches. They may offer prizes or other incentives to participate.

Investment Fraud

These cons are especially wily characters. They gain people's trust over time, and maybe even make a little money for them in the process. But that's just the "setup" for a once-in-a-lifetime opportunity to make a killing with little or no risk. Just send cash and wait for your ship to come in. Of course, it never does.

These guys use the telephone, the mails, print advertising, referrals from other investors who were paid large profits, and nice offices that look legit. They offer land sales, timeshares, commodities and futures trading, the penny stock market, rare coins in gold and silver, limited partnerships in oil and gas deals, movie deals, and the list goes on.

Don't ever invest in anything without checking it out. Legitimate limited partnerships, for example, require that an "offering memorandum" be prepared. Among other things, this document provides detailed information on the investment, including the risks involved. There are also strict guidelines on investment eligibility. So if you're considering an investment, get informed advice from a reputable investment advisor.

Health Products Fraud

The fountain of youth, the elixir of life, the cure for cancer, instant weight loss schemes, bogus arthritis remedies, baldness remedies—it's a long list. Health fraud cons are nothing more than quacks who provide easy answers to complex problems. They sell false hope.

Like all cons, they don't discriminate. Everyone is a potential target. But the elderly can be especially vulnerable because their health may be failing and traditional treatments may not be working to their satisfaction or may be too expensive. Don't be duped by false claims. Check with your doctor or appropriate professional if you are considering one of these products.

The Federal Trade Commission (FTC) has implemented tough new regulations to help enforce the telemarketing industry and help you distinguish between a fraud and an honest sales call. If you choose to talk to a salesperson on the phone and they don't follow the guidelines below, then you may be in for trouble.

Know Your Rights:
- A salesperson must tell you up front the company's name, that it's a sales call, and what is being sold. The caller cannot pretend to be doing a poll or conducting market research to get you hooked.
- Telemarketers cannot call before eight A.M. or after nine P.M. If you ask to be

removed from their list, they must comply. If they call again, they've broken the law. It's illegal for a telemarketer to misrepresent any information, including facts about their goods or services, earning potential, profitability, risk or liquidation of an investment, or the nature of a prize in a prize-promotion scheme.

- If you have won a free prize, you cannot be asked to pay anything for it. Free is free! It's illegal for a telemarketer to withdraw money from your checking account without your expressed, verifiable authorization. They can't make you buy something or say that a purchase will improve your chance to win. You cannot be asked to pay in advance for services to be delivered at a later time. Advance-fee loans are promised by shady operators who claim they can guarantee you a loan for a fee—ranging from $100 to several thousand dollars, paid in advance.

- "Credit repair" companies can't claim that, for a fee, they can change or erase accurate negative information from your credit report. They can't! Don't fall for it.

- One popular scam run by "recovery room" operators has the caller offering to recoup the money lost in a prior scam. These repeat targets have the dubious distinction of being included on "sucker lists." These lists are often exchanged or sold between con artists. So remember the old adage: Fool me once, shame on you. Fool me twice, shame on me.

The FCC does not have jurisdiction over not-for-profit organizations, so watch out for the bogus charity call too.

Con artists that use the phone have lists and computer technology and they can charm the socks off you. Remember, a snake that changes colors is still a snake. So how do you know if the call is legit or not? If the caller resorts to high-pressure tactics, it's a scam! They want you to make a decision right then and there. And they want that credit card number now!

But there are no absolutes. Sometimes they will "hook" you with a small deal that involves a modest investment, perhaps $25 or so. There may even be a modest return of some sort. But once the caller has gained your confidence, the stakes can go up quickly. Don't fall for it.

If you have even the slightest doubt about a telephone offer, wait until you can get information in writing and check it out. And if you're not convinced by now that these scams can be very tempting, try this story on for size.

LEONA SMITH

One evening Leona, a bright, well-spoken woman in her seventies, received a phone call. The call was from a man who identified himself as Tim MacGyver. He was friendly and enthusiastic and he had thrilling news for her.

He said he was from Publisher's Clearinghouse and told her she had won second prize—a check for $100,000—and Ed McMahon—"Yes, that Ed McMahon"—would show up on her doorstep with the money in about three weeks. Why was he telling her this? Well, he assumed she had seen the TV commercials—with the cameras and reporters—and he didn't want her to have a heart attack when Ed came calling.

And what did she need to do? Absolutely nothing except dress casually, act surprised when McMahon showed up, and, most important, not tell anyone else. If she did, he warned, the surprise would be ruined and the credibility of Publisher's Clearinghouse put in question, and she wouldn't want that on her conscience, would she?

Tim also mentioned, rather casually, that she could reduce the taxes on her winnings if she would just prepay the taxes by sending a cashier's check for $5,900 to Leland Industries, the accounting division of Publisher's Clearinghouse.

There was, of course, no Leland Industries. It was just a front for a fraudulent tele-marketing scheme run by a con artist named John Weaver operating out of Garden City, Michigan. Before federal authorities caught on to Weaver's scheme, he had worked his magic on dozens of victims, mostly elderly, across the country.

He was one of several con artists who searched a packet of CD-ROMs containing a national telephone directory, available at stores for under $100. And what did they do with this information? They targeted first names popular with an older generation—such as Mildred, Bertha, and Leona—figuring most would be elderly. They were—and many got taken!

So watch out. And if you are victimized, report it. It is estimated that 50 to 90 percent of all cons go unreported because people are too embarrassed or too afraid to report them.

Chapter 10

SPOTTING THE WOLF IN SHEEP'S CLOTHING

Dangerous obsessions such as stalking, serial killing, and romantic con games can be traumatic and even deadly. But we don't always know how often they occur because many of these crimes go unreported. The stalker and serial killer are not your average mugger or car thief. These guys are smooth, cold, and calculating, and many are charming. They have a complex plan and they'll get close to you and then make the hit. You won't see these guys running down the street with some lady's purse—they're too smart for that.

The Stalker

Unfortunately, tragic incidents such as stalking occur in cities and towns all over America. Stalking is nothing short of mental terrorism and it happens a lot more than you might think. It is estimated that one in twenty American women will become the victim of a stalker, and in two-thirds of these cases the stalker is the ex-husband or ex-lover. Their motive: retribution, driven by love, anger, and rage.

At the core of every stalking is this: persistence. These guys are relentless. They do not give up. And too often the results are tragic. A stalking case is one of the toughest crimes the police deal with because these guys just keep coming. The laws have got to be tough—to get to these guys before the problem escalates to violence. **The stalker's motive is retribution, driven by love, anger, and rage. And at the core of it all is this: persistence.**

KATHLEEN GALLAGHER

In the early eighties, Kathleen Gallagher was a popular student and cheerleader at UCLA. Her California lifestyle seemed almost perfect, until one November night when she was at home with her parents.

Kathleen received a strange phone call that night from a guy who said he went to college with her. She didn't recognize his name and didn't think she knew him.

Through the course of the conversation, she realized that there was something disturbing about him. So she hung up. The very next day she started receiving phone calls every five minutes for a period of four hours. There were hang-ups. And by the end of that four-hour period she recognized the voice and realized that it was some guy she had gone to high school with.

The guy, Lawrence Stagner, didn't stop with the phone calls. Later that night he waited in the bushes and lunged at Kathleen when she got home with a date. He ran off, but he wasn't finished, not by any means.

He called once and said, "I have 180 rounds of ammunition. Tell the big guy I'm going to kill him." Stagner also said that Kathleen wouldn't make it back to UCLA.

Stagner wasn't kidding about the 180 rounds of ammo. He was arrested. His punishment was forty-eight hours of psychiatric hold. When Kathleen came home from college four months later, Stagner was there. When she moved to Marina Del Rey in 1983, Stagner was there. In 1986, Kathleen moved in with her fiancé in Menlo Park and Stagner tracked her down there too.

He showed up at her door one night delivering pizza. Stagner continued to show up wherever Kathleen went. She contacted the police each time. She documented the sightings until she felt she had a case that would stand up in court. In January 1990, Stagner was given four months in jail. That was the first of several short stints in jail. Each time he got out and each time he came back.

Kathleen was frightened that he would show up at any moment. One day she was listening to the answering machine and he was standing behind her with a knife. For the next thirty minutes she was held hostage in her own house. Her mother called and when she asked Kathleen a question, Kathleen answered with a completely unrelated thought. Kathleen's mother figured out that Kathleen was signaling her and called the police.

The police surrounded the house and after several hours, Stagner brought Kathleen out the front door at gunpoint. Distracted by several officers, Stagner let his guard down and one of the officers told Kathleen to run. She did. The negotiations then went on for hours. Stagner threatened to kill himself but eventually gave himself up. He was tried, convicted, and sent to prison.

Kathleen was instrumental in getting the country's first anti-stalking bill enacted. Since that time, over forty states have enacted similar laws. These new laws make stalking a felony and allow police the leeway to arrest the stalker before the victim is physically attacked.

MARGARET CHENEY

Margaret Cheney's story is another example. It's a case of someone she loved turning from husband and father to abuser and stalker. Margaret adored her three children and was a valuable member of the management team of Occidental Oil Company. A graduate of Oklahoma State, she married Gary Cheney in 1987. The psychological abuse began right away.

Gary was so charming when they first met. He swept Margaret off her feet. The first instance of verbal abuse was on their wedding night. Then he wanted to control every minute of Margaret's day. The first time he hit Margaret, it was a complete shock. Margaret thought it could never happen to someone like her. Gary, of course, sent flowers to her office and promised it would never happen again. But it did. It just kept getting worse.

When Margaret couldn't take it any longer, she took the children and moved into a women's shelter. But Gary still persisted. An order of protection from the court didn't do any good. He still followed her.

One morning, Margaret was driving the kids to day care and Gary was sitting in the car right next to her with a gun pointed at her head.

The police arrested Gary four times for violating the protective order, but he didn't spend one hour in jail. Once they fined him fifty dollars. The next night he broke into the house and knocked Margaret down a flight of stairs—in front of the kids. He held a gun to her head and choked her until she promised to take him back. What could she do? He was going to shoot her. When she called the police they said they'd book him on felony assault, but then they gave him four days to turn himself in. Another of Margaret's concerns was the safety of her children.

Before this four-day period was up, Gary Cheney made his move. He waited for Margaret after she finished work. Leaving her office, Margaret took the elevator to the parking garage and headed for her car. She had worked late and there was no one around. Suddenly Gary appeared from behind a pillar. He confronted Margaret and verbally threatened her. Then he pulled a gun. Margaret made a run for it but he chased her up the inside ramp of the garage and fired three times. She didn't have a chance. She died right there on the cold concrete inches away from her car. The police found her car keys next to the body.

Gary Cheney was arrested, tried, and found guilty of first-degree murder. He is currently appealing the death penalty. And he's trying to block the adoption of their three kids.

Stopping the Stalker

First, you need to be able to identify any menacing signs. For example, if you say no to one of his demands, he gets enraged. The rage turns to threats, often violent threats. Second, he will exhibit wild mood swings and start snooping into your private life—where you go, what you do, who you are seeing. He'll think, "If I get rid of the other guy, she'll come back to me." Even if there is no other guy! Third, he'll turn up uninvited at work, home, or while you're out with friends.

Contact the police immediately at the first incident and report all subsequent violations of the law. Get a copy of the stalking law in your state, then you'll know what you're dealing with. Each state is different and some laws are much tougher than others.

When it comes to confronting him, make your rejection final. Tell him straight out, "I'm not interested in you any longer and that's not going to change." Once you do that, there can be no negotiation. None. The biggest mistake you can make is to negotiate with this guy because he'll promise to change.

But you're tough and you'll say, "No. It's over because I don't trust your judgment." Make it clear you are ending the relationship because of his actions, not because of some other relationship.

If he does become a problem, you can alter your routine so it's harder for him to track you down. Leave for work at a different time. Take an alternate route. Change your phone number to one that is unlisted. And document everything—this is very important.

Save letters, phone messages, keep a personal diary, confide in a friend, and fill out police reports every time this guy violates the law. If his behavior continues or he is threatening you, you will need a restraining order and that requires some documentation. When you get the restraining order, don't warn this guy off with it by waving it in his face. That can lead to confrontation and you don't want that.

Finally, work with authorities to get a conviction. That means going to court. And, if it is not the law in your state, support legislation that enables the police to act if there's a threat instead of reacting to a violent act.

Profiles of Serial Killers

Serial killers are the great white sharks of the criminal world. Considering our population, there aren't very many of them and they don't strike very often. But when they do, it's cold, calculating, and vicious. As difficult as it is to deal with a stalker known to the victim, there is one other kind of stalker that is even more ominous: the unknown stalker.

When serial killers strike, it's cold and calculating and vicious.

Over the past twenty-five years, the FBI has spent a great deal of time studying serial killers. They've interviewed hundreds of them. Fortunately, your chances of ever facing one of these guys are slim. There are only about thirty-five of them loose in the country at any one time. But that's thirty-five too many!

In its research, the FBI has found striking similarities among serial killers. Most are white males in their twenties and thirties, from middle-class homes. Many were sexually abused as children and they are typically loners. They also have trouble maintaining any kind of ongoing relationship.

THEODORE "TED" BUNDY

Bundy was a striking contrast to the "homicidal maniac" that most people imagine. He was handsome, self-assured, politically ambitious, and successful with women. His private demons drove him to extremes of violence that made the worst of the modern "slasher" films seem weak by comparison.

He posed a danger to the pretty, dark-haired women who became his victims. He began his killing spree in Seattle, Washington, and moved to Utah, Colorado, and Florida. In Florida he raped and killed two college girls. Detectives discovered bite marks on the corpses, which were evidence of Bundy's fervor at the moment of the kill. He was captured in Pensacola, Florida, a short time later. Calm and collected, Bundy mounted his own defense but the evidence against him was overwhelming. He was convicted of multiple murders; and after ten years of appeals, he was executed in Florida's electric chair in February 1989. In his last interview, he confessed to a total of forty-five murders.

JOHN WAYNE GACY

Gacy was known as the Killer Clown. The son of an alcoholic, he grew up doubting his own masculinity. Gacy appeared to be a model citizen. He was married but shocked his wife and friends when he was convicted of coercing a young restaurant employee into homosexual acts.

After serving eighteen months in prison and gettting a divorce, he moved back to Chicago, where he established himself as a successful contractor and model citizen yet again. He was active in politics and once posed for photos with President Jimmy Carter. He also performed as "Pogo the Clown" at children's parties and charity benefits.

His killing spree began on January 3, 1972. In his search for prey, Gacy would stroll the streets of Chicago for hustlers and runaways. He made friends with young boys and then brought them to his home for "tricks" and "magic handcuffs." His grand finale involved a rope trick which ended in strangulation. Gacy would then bury his victim in the crawlspace beneath his suburban home.

Before his spree was over, Gacy's lot would yield twenty-eight bodies, with five more recovered from rivers nearby. After an intense police surveillance, Gacy was finally stopped. While in custody, he tried to blame his activities on an alter ego named Jack. Gacy was found guilty and executed by lethal injection.

JEFFREY LIONEL DAHMER

This guy started early. At age ten, Dahmer was experimenting with dead animals, decapitating rodents, and bleaching chicken bones with acid. In June 1978, he crossed the line from morbidity to murder, killing a hitchhiker whom he had taken home for a drink and some laughs. When the victim tried to leave, Dahmer crushed his skull with a barbell, strangled him, then dismembered and buried his corpse.

These acts became his trademark. Over the next eleven years, Dahmer was in and out of jail and in 1987 his murderous ways began in earnest. Between 1987 and 1991, he murdered sixteen more young men. One intended victim escaped and led police to Dahmer's apartment. The remains of eleven victims were found in acid vats and inside the refrigerator. Dahmer was sentenced to life in prison without possibility of parole. In November 1994, he was murdered by a fellow inmate.

Like many of their kind, these three serial killers did indeed look and act very normal. They were charming enough to quickly establish a trusting relationship with their victims.

KEN TOLERTON

Ken Tolerton of Akron, Ohio, was certainly cut from this mold. His case did not receive the media attention of someone like Ted Bundy but he was just as much a stone-cold killer. Like Ted Bundy, Tolerton was intelligent and outgoing. He was the president of his high school ski club, president of Junior Achievement, a member of the Camera Club. Most of his classmates thought he would head to New York after graduation and become a professional photographer. But Ken Tolerton had a darker side.

In 1976, Janelle Lane was Tolerton's first intended victim. After finishing some shopping, she was leaving a parking lot in her car when Tolerton suddenly appeared. She slammed on the brakes to avoid hitting him. He walked up to her car and pointed to her back tire. Janelle rolled down her window a few inches to hear what he was saying. Tolerton told her she had a flat tire. Since he looked like a nice guy and his demeanor was not threatening, Janelle opened the car door to check out her tire. At that point, Tolerton pulled a gun on her and forced her back into the car. He jumped in the backseat and told her to drive. A nearby shopper saw the entire incident. In a gutsy move (I don't recommend anyone doing this, though it worked here), he grabbed his son's toy gun out of the backseat of his car and sprinted toward Janelle's vehicle. He said he was a police officer and told Janelle to get out of the car. Then he pointed the toy pistol at Tolerton. They faced off. Tolerton backed down and was arrested by the real police.

Ken Tolerton was sentenced to fifteen years for kidnapping and fifteen years for felonious assault. Two months later, however, he was released.

Tolerton was back on the streets. In 1980, he was seen walking through the woods on a bitter-cold night in Englewood, Colorado. A police officer, on routine patrol, noticed Tolerton wandering and told him to call it a night. Tolerton made his exit, hopped in his car, and drove off.

The officer, though suspicious, had no evidence of any wrongdoing but he did make note of the license plate number as the car sped away. Then he did some poking around in the woods and was startled to find a naked body. It was Donna Waugh. She had been raped, stabbed, and strangled. The officer immediately notified dispatch and told them the license plate number. Tolerton was picked up later that night and was convicted of murder. Amazingly, he served only four years of that sentence, shortened because of good behavior.

In the meantime, Janelle Lane was following Tolerton's exploits. "When he was released in 1991, he began to stalk women at bus stops," she said. "He would drive around these bus stops and observe, day after day, which women got on and which women got off."

Tolerton struck again in Denver, Colorado. This time it was a teenager, Cissy Foster. Cissy had been hitchhiking. When her body was found in a field there were no fingerprints, no tire tracks, no witnesses. But there was a trace of someone else's DNA.

An Arapahoe County sheriff's officer made the connection between the murders of Cissy Foster and Donna Waugh. A DNA comparison was ordered. Meanwhile, Tolerton remained free and was stopped on suspicion of stalking yet another woman during this time. He was even found with a butcher knife concealed under the seat of his car. But the woman did not press charges.

When the DNA results finally came back, it was a match. Tolerton was arrested immediately. To avoid the death penalty, he pleaded guilty and was sentenced to life in prison without the possibility of parole. Tolerton is a suspect in dozens of killings across the country. But there is little evidence to prosecute.

Protecting Yourself

The most important thing to remember is that many serial killers look and act normal. They can even be charming and act rather innocent. Ted Bundy had movie-star good looks. John Wayne Gacy dressed up as a clown and was invited regularly to appear in costume at birthday parties for neighborhood children. Jeffrey Dahmer befriended young men with his nice-guy approach.

So be aware. And beware! Be smart. Be cautious. Never hitchhike. Don't trust strangers. And, of course, you are not going anywhere with someone you don't know well.

The Casanova

I call the next crime the Casanova syndrome, which is nothing more than a sophisticated con game. Many con games involve dangling some kind of bait in front of the intended victim. The bait is greed—getting something for nothing. Well, the Casanova uses a different kind of bait—love.

Every year these guys roam the country stealing women's hearts and, very often, everything they own. How many are there? That's nearly impossible to say because most victims are so ashamed of being had that they don't report the crime to police.

GIOVANNI VIGLIOTTO

Giovanni was the classic chameleon. He became whatever his mark wanted him to be. He did it with charm, a quick smile, and always with a story. The story was laced with half-truths and lies. His style never changed. He romanced lonely, middle-aged women, and offered them a first-class ride down easy street. It was a one-way trip to emotional and financial disaster. Jan Forrester was one of his victims.

At forty-four, Jan had recently relocated to the Midwest, where she worked long hours as a real estate agent. She was smart and self-sufficient. But she was no match for this smoothie.

Jan had been living in Cincinnati for about fifteen months when she met Giovanni. She thought he was the man of her dreams. It all started innocently enough. They met at a flea market. Giovanni Vigliotto introduced himself as an antique expert and offered to show her around. It was fun, and he was fun and charming.

Jan told him she was in real estate and he said he was looking to invest in a condo. They met the next day and spent a lot of time together. They were married two weeks after they met. They were so busy they didn't even have time to go get an engagement ring, so they used cigar bands for wedding rings. It seemed so romantic at the time. Giovanni promised Jan that he'd take care of her and she'd never have to work again.

Giovanni told Jan to sell her house and travel to Milwaukee with him. He said he didn't want the bank tying up her money so she got it in cash. Giovanni was so smooth that Jan trusted him completely and turned most of the cash over to him. They sold most of Jan's antiques because there would be no room for them in his house. Within thirty days of meeting him, everything Jan owned could fit inside a van.

Before the trip, they went on a shopping spree with Jan's credit cards. He told her if they were run up to the max and paid off immediately, their credit limit would be increased. Jan believed everything. After all, this was her husband.

A week after the wedding they left for Milwaukee. Jan drove her car and he drove the van with Jan's stuff in it. The first night he stopped at Indianapolis. The next morning, he went on ahead and said they would meet for lunch at a Holiday

Inn in Chicago. He called her several times and always had a different excuse—a flat tire, a call from a lawyer, you name it. Then Jan realized he wasn't coming for her at all.

She called the police and was sent to the U.S. Marshall's office. She found out the man she had married was named Fred Gyp and that he had been married eighty-three times. She was left with just seventy-four dollars in cash, three changes of clothes, a car, and a dog.

Fred Gyp, aka Giovanni Vigliotto, would zero in on his target, make his move, and be gone before most of his victims knew what hit them. They were vulnerable because they wanted to believe.

One of his wives pursued him relentlessly across America. This woman would not be denied. She caught up with him in Panama City, Florida, and had him arrested. He was found guilty of fraud and bigamy and sentenced to thirty-four years in prison.

Research Your Romeo

Information is power and when it comes to relationships, you need all the power you can get. If you're looking, you'll notice the warning signs. A con man's story will usually be full of contradictions—who he is, what he does, where he's from.

There may be significant holes in time—months, even years—that he won't discuss. He'll brush it off as a bad time in his life that he just can't talk about. He'll dance around your questions and make you feel guilty for not trusting him or for not understanding him. These guys don't waste much time when it comes to their true motive. They zero in quickly and the target will be your financial affairs. He may ask you for a temporary loan, to invest, to buy property, or to sell off assets.

Like any con, if it sounds too good to be true, it is! He may have a criminal record or he may already have a wife, or two, or several. Maybe he's up to his eyeballs in debt, with bill collectors on his tail. Maybe there are lawsuits pending. So what do you do if you're interested in some guy with this potential liability?

• Get to know the people who know him. Meet his family and friends. Arrange to meet him at his place of work and go to lunch from there. Ask for his home phone number and call him at home.

• Find out his social security number. In most states it will be on his driver's license. Then you can check him out over the phone. There are data companies that can tell you if your guy went bankrupt in Baltimore, has a lien in Louisville, or a wife in Wichita. If you tap into one of the online computer services you may be able to type in his name and find out his last residence.

- Was he ever in prison? Call the Federal Prison Locator Service at (202) 307-3126.
- "Sam Spade" may be your best ally in today's world of romance. For a few hundred bucks you can hire a private detective. But be careful. Be sure to get a referral from a friend or attorney. Most P.I.s offer a no-cost private consultation. Take advantage of it. If you choose this route, make sure the P.I. you select is experienced and licensed by the state. Whatever you do, don't rely on dating services that advertise complete background checks. Most do not even scratch the surface.

Whether you do the leg work or hire someone else to do it, prepare yourself emotionally for what you may find. These days, love can't afford to be blind.

Personals Protection

Today most singles find it increasingly difficult to balance work, family, and social lives. This is one of the reasons why many turn to personal ads as the vehicle of choice for their dating connection. While the vast majority of singles using personal ads are sincere, there are always those who are out for something more!

When you find yourself in personals territory, you need to follow some simple guidelines. If you are placing an ad or responding to one, do not give out your phone number to someone you don't know. If you do decide to meet this person, make sure it is in a public place with plenty of people around. Remember, there are a lot of crazies out there. Travel to and from the meeting place by yourself. If you're taking a cab or public transportation, don't let him know that. He may insist on driving you home and you don't want that. Not on the first date, anyway. If you decide to give him your phone number after meeting him—and I suggest you don't—give him your work number not your home number.

These guidelines should apply to women as well as men. There are many crazy ladies out there as well.

Chapter 11

RESPONDING TO RAPE

Aside from murder, rape is the most vicious crime one human being can commit against another. There is no doubt. And while there is often physical abuse involved in a rape, those wounds usually heal. The emotional and psychological wounds can last a lifetime. As a detective, I've interviewed many hundreds of rape victims and their stories all have one common thread: The attacker used sex as a weapon—to dominate and humiliate. Rape is not a sex crime, it is a crime of violence. **Rape is not a sex crime, it is a crime of violence.**

Statistics are available on this topic and they are scary. A U.S. Senate report stated that one in five women will be raped at some point in their lives. The National Crime Center and Crime Victims Research and Treatment Center in Arlington, Virginia, reports that more than 700,000 women are sexually assaulted in the United States each year. Many rapes are not even reported. Even allowing for statistical errors, these numbers are appalling.

Rape is often defined in different ways but the bottom line is this: If a person does not consent or is unable to consent to engage in sexual acts—but is forced into those acts—that's rape! There are also different definitions to describe the kinds of rape. The terms may differ, but essentially the classifications come down to three: date rape, acquaintance rape, and stranger-danger rape. In recent years, a fourth classification has emerged: domestic rape. It's been around for a long time but it was always treated differently than other forms of rape.

Kinds of Rape

Date rape is one of the most common forms of rape and involves two people who know one another, though often not well. Acquaintance rape also involves people who know one another. The distinction is that, on a date, there is an expectation of intimacy. Not a burning romance necessarily, but some level of intimacy: hand holding, dancing, sitting in a movie theater, or talking privately. (This form of rape is discussed in detail in Chapter 8, Staying Safe on Campus.)

That is not the case with acquaintance rape, where there is no expectation of intimacy. For example, a person might go out after work with a group from the office. A colleague is offered a ride home. The offer is accepted because it's convenient and saves cab fare. But this guy may have a different agenda and if that leads to forced sex, it's rape.

In stranger-danger rape, there is no expectation of contact. It just happens, often suddenly and without warning. It is usually entirely random. This form of rape is the least common but most dangerous.

The question of whether to fight back or not to fight back in a rape situation is one that is hotly debated. It's a question I'm often asked and there is no easy answer. My answer is this: Whatever you need to do to survive a rape, you've done the right thing. But you can increase the odds in your favor.

Stranger-Danger Rape

A smart plan keeps the potential rapist out and the problem is solved. Good locks and a home security system are a good start. For now, let's go right past all that and assume you are face to face with your worst nightmare: a stranger in your bedroom. Let's also assume you are alone, no child to worry about, just yourself. The decision to fight or not is a judgment call you have to make in the heat of the moment. And there is no way to second-guess these situations. If you submit and survive, you've done the right thing. But if you choose to fight, here's what you do.

You're smart, so you keep a canister of pepper spray in your nightstand drawer and a portable phone next to the bed. Fight this guy off enough to get to the pepper spray and nail him with it. That will put him out of commission and let him know you are not going to be a victim. Then grab your phone and call the police. Many phones come with an emergency button; have the police number programmed into your speed dial.

If you've got a home security system and the alarm goes off—or if you get a call from the alarm monitoring company saying that one of your basement windows has just been opened—call the police. Call them right away. In some communities, phone service is underground. In these locations the wires are more vulnerable to being cut. If your phone is dead when you try to call the police, the intruder knows you are home and is trying to make sure that you cannot call for help.

What do you do in that case? Pick up your cellular phone and call. If you keep the charger for the cell phone in your bedroom, you can find it in the dark (most chargers have little lights) and call. You can get under the bed with the phone if you have to.

Okay, what if you have no pepper spray, no phone in the bedroom, no alarm. Well, if you decide to fight, then fight as if your life is on the line—because it probably is! If fleeing is not an option and you're going to fight, go in 100 percent committed. And remember also the eyes, throat, and groin are his most vulnerable areas. Jab your fingers in his eyes, punch him in the throat, kick him in the groin. Whatever it takes. Throw a lamp or chair through the window to let your neighbors know that you are in trouble. At this point, you don't hold back. You don't want to hurt him a little—that will only make him mad. Hurt him a lot! Make sure he understands he's picked the wrong house and the wrong woman.

SHEILA BRODSKY

Sheila was confronted with a stranger in her bedroom but didn't fight back because she feared for her daughter's life. She still remembers every detail of her ordeal although the rape occurred several years ago.

After reading a story to her three-year-old daughter, Sheila tucked her into bed and went downstairs to iron. It was stuffy in the kitchen so she cracked open the window a few inches to get some fresh air. What she didn't know at the time was that she was being watched.

A short time later, she finished the ironing and went to bed. She read for a while and then went to sleep. At about eleven-thirty she was jarred awake by someone who was right on top of her. She could not see his face but she heard voices, so she knew he was not alone.

Sheila's first thought was for her daughter's safety. Her little girl was right down the hall and she was more afraid for her than for herself. Sheila was threatened with a knife to her throat. She told them they could have whatever they wanted. One guy went downstairs to get Sheila's purse. The thirteen dollars that was in the house only enraged the attackers. They beat and raped her repeatedly. In the middle of the attack, Sheila's daughter woke up. The attackers let Sheila go to soothe her daughter.

As Sheila was calming her daughter, one of the guys showed up at the door and said, "If she makes another sound you can kiss her goodbye. Now shut her up and get back down the hall." It was horrible, but Sheila thought there was nothing else she could do. Sheila felt that if she fought back, they would kill her little girl.

Anyway, when it was over Sheila wrapped herself in a sheet. The rapists took her stereo and TV and left. Sometime later Sheila managed to call the police. But it wasn't over. These things are never over! Because she can never, ever forget!

Rape victims never forget! Sheila did the right thing that night because she and her daughter survived that ordeal. She thought about fighting back but didn't. She feared for the life of her little girl and she had every reason to be afraid of these guys. After the rape, Sheila got the police involved, she went to the hospital right away, and she cooperated in the capture and conviction of the intruders.

Remember the kitchen window? Sheila opened it to let in some fresh air. And that's how these guys gained entry. But it was a narrow window and one of them had to remove his jacket to slide through. Fortunately for the police, the jacket was left behind. In one of the pockets was a business card. It wasn't his, but the guy who owned the card gave the detectives a lead.

That name matched the description Sheila Brodsky provided and she was brought to view the lineup. When you have two suspects in a lineup you need five fillers. Sheila viewed the seven-man lineup and identified one of the men. She said that she was not 100 percent sure but that if she could hear his voice, she'd be able to make a positive identification.

The rules for lineups say that if one person in the lineup is required to speak, then all participants must speak. Each of the seven men was brought to the door, one at a time. The detective then instructed each to say, "Lay down and take off your nightgown." Each man repeated the phrase. The suspect—the one Sheila was not 100 percent sure of— took his turn. Instead of saying, "Lay down and take off your nightgown," he said, "That ain't what I told her." At this point, Sheila Brodsky was sure of her attacker.

This man was questioned and he confessed to his involvement in the crime, but he was not the main guy. To save his own hide, he made a deal with the prosecutors and fingered his partner, who was also in that lineup but had not been identified.

The unidentified partner was placed in an interview room with the detective. Here's what happened:

DETECTIVE: Listen, pal. The victim has not signed a complaint against you and I'm not sure she's going to. But if you want the chance to apologize to this woman,

I'm going to let you do that. So you think about it. I'll be back in fifteen minutes.

FIFTEEN MINUTES LATER HE RETURNED.

DETECTIVE: So what do you think, pal? You going to apologize or not?

BAD GUY: I don't know, man. I'm not sure. I guess I could.

DETECTIVE: Well, you wait right in this room. She just stepped out for a cup of coffee but she'll be back in ten minutes.

> *MEANWHILE, THE DETECTIVE WENT INTO THE SQUAD ROOM AND ENLISTED THE HELP OF SEVERAL FEMALE OFFICERS. THEY CHANGED OUT OF THEIR UNIFORMS INTO STREET CLOTHES. HE ALSO RECRUITED ONE OTHER WOMAN WHO WAS AT THE STATION HOUSE THAT DAY—AN ASSISTANT STATE'S ATTORNEY.*
>
> *THE WOMEN WERE INSTRUCTED TO SIT ALL AROUND THE LARGE SQUAD ROOM AND SHEILA WAS BROUGHT OUT OF AN INTERVIEW ROOM TO JOIN THEM. THERE WERE EIGHT WOMEN IN ALL. SEVERAL OTHER DETECTIVES WERE STATIONED AT THE EXITS TO MAKE SURE THAT THE GUY DID NOT MAKE A RUN FOR IT.*

DETECTIVE: C'mon, let's go. I don't want you to ever come back to me and say you didn't have a chance to apologize.

> *THE DETECTIVE OPENED THE INTERVIEW ROOM DOOR AND HELD IT OPEN. THE SUSPECT STEPPED INTO THE LARGE OFFICE SPACE.*

DETECTIVE: Okay, now go apologize.

> *THE BAD GUY LOOKED AROUND THE ROOM AT THE WOMEN, PAUSED, AND WALKED RIGHT OVER TO SHEILA. THE DETECTIVE FOLLOWED ABOUT TWO STEPS BEHIND.*

BAD GUY: Ma'am, I'm sorry.

DETECTIVE: That ain't good enough. You're sorry for what?

BAD GUY: Ma'am, I'm sorry I raped you.

The detective then led the suspect back into the interview room and closed the door. He said, "Good job. That was not only a reverse lineup, but a confession as well. You're under arrest for rape and home invasion."

We called this the reverse lineup because the bad guy identified the victim. Of course, it's usually the other way around. And the confession held up in court! The guy who apologized was sentenced to twenty years in prison and his partner got off with six years. I know because I was that detective.

Their time in the joint will never compensate for Sheila's pain, but at least they were taken off the streets and other potential victims were spared.

Sheila Brodsky is now an active speaker against rape. "I'm a survivor, not a victim," she says. "And what I want others to understand is that if this could happen to me, it could happen to you. It can happen to anyone. In a moment of panic you need to have something to fall back on. You need to have a plan and know your options. In another situation I may have done exactly the same thing as I did, but I felt helpless and vulnerable. My daughter and I got out of this alive so that's the most important thing. We were lucky!"

Acquaintance Rape

Stranger-danger rape is often the most dangerous type of rape but there is no distinction when it comes to the emotional issues. This next story involves acquaintance rape—the rape of a teenage girl.

This is a very disturbing story. But there are some important lessons to be learned here and that's why it is included. It is a tragic example of the emotional and psychological wounds inflicted during a rape and their effects on a person and her family.

ANGIE WILTZ

Angie Wiltz was an outgoing fourteen-year-old who loved to write poems. She worked at a restaurant and agreed to babysit for her employer's son's children.

About one A.M., thirty-one-year-old Gary Etherington returned home from a night on the town with friends. He had been drinking heavily and Angie knew it. She was smart at first and declined his offer to drive her home. She never had any reason to fear Etherington but she was uncomfortable with the situation and told him she would call her aunt for a ride. Angie's aunt agreed to pick her up. But Etherington insisted that he would drive her home. Angie stuck to her guns and said no. Etherington persisted. Finally, with some fear, she called her aunt and told her she didn't need the ride after all. Angie's aunt was concerned and told her so. But Angie said she'd be fine.

Angie and Etherington got into his pickup truck and started for Angie's house. It wasn't far. But Etherington had something else in mind. He turned down a dirt road and drove to a deserted wooded area. And then he raped her. He was a big guy and Angie—only fourteen years old—could not fight him off.

When it was over, he drove her home and acted like nothing had happened. Angie was terrified and traumatized.

This was only the beginning of an ordeal that will never end for Angie's family. Angie never recovered from this vicious act. Over the next several months Angie went into a deep depression.

Her family and friends did not know how to help her. They encouraged her to see a therapist. She did. The therapist learned that Angie was taking showers three and four times a day because she felt dirty and that Angie blamed herself for the rape.

There were times during this period when the old Angie emerged, but they were few. Her tailspin continued and her poems, once filled with hope and sunshine, turned ominous and dark. "You can feel your lungs gasp for air. The slit in your wrist wasn't a dare. I'll leave this world without a simple goodbye. Not even my friends will cry. They'll look for me in hell, but it's better than life's evil spell. The doctors will try to make me survive, but it's better being dead than alive."

Unfortunately, that poem became her epitaph. Almost one year to the day after the rape, Angie left her home, walked into the woods and into the night. She threw a rope over a tree and hanged herself.

Gary Etherington was tried and convicted of rape but got off with a short sentence and served an even shorter time in prison. He claimed Angie came on to him.

No Means No

The most important thing you can do is to empower your child to say no to forced affection from anyone—family or friend. Teach them to do it respectfully but firmly. Start this empowerment at a very young age. Why? Because if a child is taught that they can say no to forced affection from family, they will say no to anyone.

When the child is a teenager, they will be tougher and will know how to handle tough situations. This means that even in a situation like Angie's, when this guy came home drunk in the middle of the night, no means NO! That's it. End of discussion. Angie was intimidated into going with Etherington that night and it eventually cost her her life. She's fourteen, he's thirty-one. She's a kid in the wrong place at the wrong time.

DESIREE WASHINGTON

Desiree Washington was flattered by the attention she was getting from Mike Tyson, the heavyweight boxing champion of the world. She was eighteen years old and a beauty pageant contestant, he was charming and famous. Because he was a celebrity, she assumed she was safe in his company. Wrong! According to the jury.

After a pageant event one evening, Desiree went for a ride in Tyson's limo and joined him in his hotel room. Soon after their arrival, he became aggressive and demanded sex. She refused so he forced himself on her.

It was days after that Washington summoned the courage to report the rape. She knew, by doing so, she would become part of a media circus. She also knew her reputation would be put on trial along with Mike Tyson's. In a highly publicized trial in Indianapolis, it came down to Tyson's word against Washington's. He admitted to having sex with her but said it was consensual. She said she was raped. The jury believed Washington. Tyson was given a six-year prison sentence. He served three. The verdict was considered a landmark because of the place and circumstances in which it was committed. Washington had willingly gone to Tyson's hotel room.

This was a case where the jury upheld a woman's right to say no, regardless of what may have been compromising circumstances. The message was this: Just because a woman makes a mistake in judgment doesn't mean she is a willing accomplice in her own rape. It doesn't matter where or when the rape occurred. Even if a woman has been intimate with a man in the past, and obviously attracted to him, she has the right to say no at any point in time. And no matter how aroused this guy may be, he has no right to force sex on her. That's the bottom line.

Protecting Yourself Against Rape

If you find yourself in a compromising predicament, your main objective should be to get out of there. If he is big and strong, you may not be able to keep him off you. So if clawing and kicking and screaming don't work, here's a last resort that should work.

In a date rape or acquaintance rape, the guy will usually want to kiss you. That is less the case in a stranger-danger rape, but it sometimes happens. If he does try to kiss you, let him. Kiss him just long enough to get hold of his lower lip. Then bite down hard on that lower lip until your teeth meet.

This will create the distraction you need to make your move. But you'd better be prepared to get out of there. Fast! Because you are going to do some serious damage to this guy and he is going to be in a great deal of pain. He's also going to be mad as hell.

So this kind of action is not something you are going to do without some serious thought. It's not something you figure out in the heat of the moment. It's something you consciously decide you are going to do if you have to do it. And only if you have to do it. It's part of your plan.

Dressing Defensively

No woman asks or deserves to be raped, no matter what the circumstances may be. But there are things women can do—especially in the areas of dress and attitude—that can minimize the risk of rape.

A provocative manner and clothing are every woman's right in our society. These things are a matter of choice. However, right or wrong, they can also send the wrong message. If you avoid revealing attire, you avoid drawing unwanted attention to your body. And that can help keep you safe. (Remember in Chapter 5? Save the close-fitting exercise clothes for the gym. Well, the same principle applies here.) A no-nonsense, smartly dressed business women will be treated with more respect than the same woman wearing sexier clothing. Everybody has a right to dress the way they feel most comfortable. However, the more prudent person would not walk down a dark alley in a tough neighborhood at two A.M., naked, carrying a fistful of twenty-dollar bills. You are responsible for yourself, so be smart and don't look for trouble.

Body language is also important. Remember that the lions never go after the swiftest or strongest antelope in the herd. It's the weak one they eat for dinner. If you walk around with your head down like you're looking for loose change, you are more likely to be considered an easy target. It's not how tough you are, it's how tough he thinks you are. So look tough!

Your tone of voice and your verbal response are other things to consider. Since most rapes are committed by someone known to the victim, you may initially be surprised when the behavior of an acquaintance turns aggressive. If it does, you need to treat him as if he were a total stranger. You need to look him straight in the eyes and be very clear where you stand. And don't worry about offending him. In a firm tone of voice say, "Listen, you are out of line and I am not interested. Now leave me alone." That's it. End of discussion.

Alcohol can also be a large factor involved in rape. So be smart and be careful when it comes to the use and misuse of alcohol. Don't drink so much that you can't control your actions and don't be near someone who is drinking irresponsibly.

If You Are Raped

If you are raped, or if someone you know is raped, here's what to do:

- Tell your parents or a trusted friend at once—you need that support.
- Call the police immediately. This improves the odds they will nail this guy.
- Don't change clothes or bathe. This may be very hard to do but it's important.

  Your body may be the evidence needed to get a conviction.

Remember, reporting the crime does not mean you have to prosecute, but these guys need to be locked up, so I urge any victim of sexual assault to prosecute the offender. That means this guy is not going to do to someone else what he did to you. We need rape victims to come forward to get these creeps off the street. Most of them will strike again—and again!

Many states have prosecutors specifically assigned to sexual assault cases. If not, insist on a prosecutor experienced in rape cases.

Join a support group for rape victims and talk about your experience as soon as you are able. The hospital will have the number of a rape crisis center. Get some professional help from a counselor or therapist to deal with the emotional trauma. The emotional wounds are there, even if you think they're not. And finally, whatever you do, don't blame yourself. You didn't provoke this crime. You didn't ask to be raped. It's not your fault. It's his fault, it's his crime. Let's make him pay!

There are no winners in a violent confrontation, only survivors. If you are violently assaulted you may be affected for months, maybe years, after the attack. Experts agree that you should not bury the memory. How you deal with the aftermath of a violent confrontation depends on how you feel about your reaction during the incident; how others feel about what you did; and whether you are aware of the effects of post-violence trauma.

The important thing is to deal with it. It wasn't your fault. You didn't ask to be targeted. And if you survived, you did the right thing—whatever it was. If you weren't prepared, don't beat yourself up; learn from it and be prepared in case there is a next time.

To turn this around, we need to make people aware, we need tough laws against these creeps, a willingness on the part of victims to report and prosecute the crime, and, perhaps most important, education.

Many women's organizations have been fighting this battle for years. Recent efforts have focused on four areas of rape-law reform: the definition of the crime, rules of evidence, statutory age, and penalties. Some of the results are promising.

In 1995, the American Medical Association (AMA) released its first-ever sexual assault treatment guidelines. In that report the AMA calls sexual assault the "silent-violent epidemic." New legislation has significantly improved the processing of rape cases, which can drag on for years in the courts.

Domestic Rape

The fourth type of rape that is prevalent is domestic rape. This means the rape of a spouse or live-in partner. One of the reasons this is an issue is the common public belief that sexual gratification is a right of marriage. Consensual sex is. A husband has the right to engage in sex with his wife only if she consents. Any sexual activity between two people—married or not—where one partner is not consenting or is unable to consent is rape. In some cases, sexual abuse may even be accepted as a necessity by the victim. And while efforts to stop the rise in domestic violence have increased through both private and governmental initiatives, the results remain grim.

The issue is complicated by the fact that it is almost impossible to determine the extent of the problem. Some studies indicate that as many as half of all marriages are violent at some level. Fifty percent of all injured women receiving treatment in emergency rooms are there because of violent relationships. It is estimated that somewhere between 25 and 40 percent of all homicides result from violent relationships in the home. And 25 percent of all white female suicides and 50 percent of all black female suicides are linked to domestic violence. We really don't know for sure how many women are affected. What matters is that the problem exists. And something should be done about it.

The problem is not limited to "battered women," or "battered wives." It is really partner abuse. And it is not limited to marital status, sexual orientation, or even gender, although the vast majority of battering cases involve male offenders and female victims.

What Is Battering?

Battering begins with behavior like threats, name calling, violence in the presence of the woman (e.g., punching a fist through a wall), and/or damage to objects or pets. Every fifteen seconds the crime of battering occurs. It may escalate to restraining, pushing, slapping, and pinching. And finally, the actual battering may include punching, kicking, biting, and sexual assault. It may become life-threatening, such as choking or breaking bones.

Not all battering is physical. Battering includes emotional abuse, economic abuse, sexual abuse, threats, intimidation, and isolation. These are all used to maintain fear, intimidation, and power.

The victims of battering often suffer injuries that are not as apparent as those in stranger-to-stranger crimes. For example, a common way to abuse women is to hit them in the area between the shoulders and the upper thighs, where such injuries are usually not visible.

Emotional injuries may parallel those suffered by victims of stranger violence but they can also go beyond that. There is shock, denial, and disbelief in either case. When it involves partners, the disbelief is often chronic. "This isn't happening to me." "It is going to get better." "It won't happen again."

It's an emotional roller coaster for the victim. For many, the anger so common in victims of stranger violence may take years to surface. There is fear, terror, and often confusion. "Why is this happening to me?"

Psychological abuse can cause a steady deterioration of self-esteem that may lead to despair. This is further compounded by isolation—demands that the partner separate from support systems such as family and friends. There will be no one to turn to for support or comfort. The abuse may take the form of humiliation, or deliberate destruction of sentimental belongings or even pets.

Partner abuse always originates within the person who is the offender. And the old adage "like father, like son" is especially relevant here. Because most violence is learned behavior, children who observe violence or are beaten are more likely to exhibit these same behaviors as adults or accept the violence because they think it's normal.

It is a pattern of behavior with the effect of establishing power and control over another person through fear and intimidation, often including the threat or use of violence. Battering happens when batterers believe they are entitled to control their partners, when violence is considered permissible, when violence will produce the desired effect or prevent a worse one, and when the benefits outweigh the consequences.

Who Are the Victims?

There is no stereotype for a typical battered woman. They include rural and urban women of all religious, ethnic, economic, and educational backgrounds, of varying ages, physical abilities, and lifestyles.

It is estimated by some sources that more than 50 percent of all women will experience physical violence in an intimate relationship, and for most of those women, the battering will be regular and ongoing.

The behaviors routinely identified in these situations are generally put in four categories: alcohol and drug abuse, power and control, "concentration camp" syndrome, and cycle-of-violence theory.

ALCOHOL AND DRUG ABUSE: There is no conclusive evidence that links violence with alcohol and other drugs. But I can tell you from experience that an overwhelming number of cases involve these substances. And too often the victim feels that if the batterer would only stop the behavior, things would get better. Many victims, hoping to find some logical and treatable reason for the violence, tend to excuse the abusiveness when alcohol or drugs are involved.

POWER AND CONTROL: The lines have blurred from the traditional male/female marital relationship where the power was with the husband. However, in spite of women working outside the home—and enjoying an increasing professional independence—many women have little economic independence. This may be exploited to the point of abusive behavior. The batterer often has low self-esteem and turns his home into a private fiefdom, using violence as the ultimate form of control and expression of power.

"CONCENTRATION CAMP" SYNDROME: This is a phrase coined by many victim services and refers to the desire of the batterer to humiliate, degrade, and eventually destroy his partner. He will construct a domestic environment where the victim constantly must prove her worth: for example, maintaining a spotless home and serving dinner on time.

Since the batterer may feel a sense of frustration in his own life, he becomes immersed in an emotional spiral, where his own self-control goes down and violence goes up. Drug and alcohol abuse are often involved here as well.

CYCLE-OF-VIOLENCE THEORY: This refers to the impact of stress upon the relationship. Stress can be caused by economic, job, family, social, or other conditions which can create tension. The batterer reacts to that tension with violence. It often starts slow and later explodes into a violent confrontation and then is followed by a period of remorse, where forgiveness is sought. He may send flowers or candy and promises to never do it again. Of course, those promises are empty. In fact, in many cases the honeymoon phase becomes less and less frequent and the violence becomes more intense.

Victims remain in abusive relationships for many reasons: fear, lack of perceived alternatives, love, and undying optimism—optimism that things will change. The victim is faced with an experience quite similar to that of prisoners of war: fear, isolation, and abuse mixed with an occasional indulgence. Unfortunately, society has traditionally tolerated such behavior based on historical, social, cultural, and religious factors.

Combating Domestic Violence

Why doesn't she just leave? She's crazy to stay with that jerk! What's wrong with her? These are common questions and comments directed to victims of abuse. Many victims make choices that seem confusing, contradictory, or even crazy to others. For example, they go back to the abuser after a period of separation, or refuse to testify in a criminal case.

Why do they do this? Because they believe that true safety is not possible, so they focus instead on survival. It's important that we recognize these coping strategies for what they are. This means we stop blaming the victim. It's time to stop asking, what's wrong with her? And start asking, what's wrong with him?

In order to fight domestic abuse, we must begin with the community and the criminal justice system. There are no easy answers to this problem but here are some of the key considerations.

THE COMMUNITY: Violence-prevention education programs should be established in schools from kindergarten through high school. Children need to be taught non-violent solutions to resolve conflicts. Religious institutions need to take a leadership role in urging a stand against domestic abuse. Shelters need to be available for victims of abusive situations, with follow-up educational, financial, and employment assistance. And programs for abusers must be better developed and sustained. We need to take action and save the people around us from these abusive monsters.

THE CRIMINAL JUSTICE SYSTEM: Domestic violence should be clearly defined as a crime and police officers need to be adequately trained to deal with intervention and arrest, if appropriate. Prosecutors should establish a separate unit to deal with domestic violence issues; and prosecutors specially trained in the dynamics of family violence should be assigned these cases. They should be experts at dealing with photographs of injuries and documenting the history of all types of abuse, and knowledgable about battered women's syndrome and post-traumatic stress disorder.

If you, or someone you know, is a victim of domestic abuse, you've got to report it and get help. The National Coalition Against Domestic Violence, in Denver, Colorado, serves as a national information and referral center for the general public, the media, battered women and their children, and other agencies and organizations. The NCADV can also direct you to more than 2,500 shelters and service programs in existence today. They provide programs with information and technical assistance to address the special needs of battered women. Call: (303) 839-1852.

Chapter 12

VIOLENCE
IN THE WORKPLACE

In my line of work, danger is part of the job. Police officers know that at the outset. And we learn to never let down our guard. Even the routine, like stopping a motorist for speeding, could turn explosive if the guy has something to hide. The police are always prepared. We look out for each other. We know how to respond when bad things start to happen. Our employers—the law enforcement agencies—go to great lengths to teach us how to prepare and how to stay safe.

Most employers are good at preparing employees for dangers inherent in the job. Warehouse workers are taught how to avoid back injury, hospital workers learn to guard against infection, and mail carriers are instructed on the art of dodging unfriendly dogs. But preparing employees for acts of violence is a matter that most employers ignore.

I doubt that Bonnie Serpico and her employer, a data-processing firm, were overly concerned about her personal safety working the night shift in suburban Chicago. They were more likely worried about the health effects of sitting at a computer. But a masked gunman entered the office through a locked front door and attempted to rape Bonnie and co-worker Lori Rowe. Bonnie was shot to death trying to escape. Lori survived multiple gunshot wounds. The murderer gained entry using a master key he had obtained years earlier while working on a construction crew at the building. No one had ever thought to change the locks. This was a crime that could have been avoided.

If you are not in a management position, you may feel powerless to do anything about this lack of preparedness. But you are responsible for your own safety! It's up to you to take the initiative.

Consider this: The Occupational Safety and Health Administration (OSHA) reports that workplace homicides are the third leading cause of job-related deaths and the number one cause of death for women on the job. It's your responsibility to make your environment safe.

Violence in the workplace generally arises in four different ways:

1. As a consequence of a robbery or theft. This occurs in businesses that have cash on hand—banks, fast-food stops, convenience stores, liquor stores, and other retail establishments that keep late-night hours. The bad guy is armed and nervous. He may not intend to harm anyone, but things don't always go as planned and he may overreact. When that happens, innocent employees often wind up dead.

2. Spillover from a domestic dispute. The dispute has probably been going on for some time. It could be about money, kids, jealousy, or infidelity—any of the things that men and women quarrel about. One scenario may be a separation or divorce that leads to stalking. He can't get to her at home so he goes where she is accessible—at work. Sometimes innocent employees are caught in the crossfire.

3. Violence specifically directed at the employer. The bad guy could be a current or former employee, or even a customer. The target might be the company as a whole or certain executives, managers, or co-workers. The trigger to violent behavior could be a job termination or a series of bad performance reviews. This goof places the blame within the company and decides the only solution is violence. Once again, innocent employees are victimized.

4. Acts of terrorism. Terrorists use fear as a motivator to create awareness of their cause and to evoke a political response. They're trying to scare as many people as possible. Therefore, they tend to target governmental or high-profile facilities.

Employee violence is one act of violence that you can prevent. This constitutes inside threats, where a fellow employee is the source of the violence. The reason you can prevent these acts is that there are generally warning signs before the violence happens.

Most violent episodes start with a traumatic experience, such as termination or a series of negative performance reviews. The individual experiences great anxiety and puts blame on the company or the people involved.

This can lead to internal conflict. The individual's thinking becomes self-centered and focuses on the problem without regard to other concerns. Generally, a period of internal conflict ensues before the individual commits the act of violence.

According to the experts, the persons most likely to get violent in the workplace have a tendency to be loners. They have few relationships with co-workers. Or they are people whose lives are centered around their work, making them more likely to lose control if their job is in jeopardy.

Here are some telltale warnings of a troubled and potentially dangerous co-worker:

- Person commands increasing attention of supervisors and co-workers.
- Inconsistent work patterns and decreased productivity.
- Lower level of concentration—forgets job instructions, misses deadlines, forgets to bring necessary items to work, etc.
- Stress—shows signs of anger, anxiety, mood swings, and nervousness.
- Exaggerated personality traits—quiet people withdraw further, loud people get louder.
- Signs of drug or alcohol abuse.

In many cases, the individual in question makes a threat prior to taking action. That is the most important warning sign—don't ignore it.

You may have been unsure about the seriousness of the situation beforehand, but once you hear a threat there should be no doubt. It's clearly time to let the appropriate authorities know about it. Be alert for the telltale signs of danger, and get involved—take action before the problem escalates to violence.

Regardless of where you work, you could be a victim of one or more of these types of workplace violence. The good news is that there are steps employers and employees can take to reduce their exposure.

Your employer is responsible for building the first line of defense. Some do a good job of this—others not so good. Most large companies generally have a security department. Security in the smaller firms may lie with the general manager or owner. There's almost always room for improvement.

Most companies would rather invest in things that are going to increase sales. Too often, companies get serious about security after there has been a robbery or act of violence. To prevent this, you can influence your employer's security program by speaking up, asking intelligent questions, making suggestions, and offering to help.

Do You Work in a Safe Place?

The following checklist will help you determine if you work in a safety-conscious environment.

√ Are all outside points of entrance (i.e., doors, gates, loading docks) secured with locks, alarms, closed-circuit surveillance cameras, or security guards?

√ Is the visitor reception area controlled by a receptionist who is trained on security measures?

√ Do all visitors require an escort? Are customers in a retail establishment restricted from employee areas?

√ If the company is housed in a large facility or a multi-office complex, is access to the facility controlled by ID badges, sign in/out procedures, and restricted hours for visitors?

√ Are parking lots well lit and guarded? Is there an escort service available?

√ Are restrooms kept locked to prevent an outsider from gaining access?

√ Is incoming mail pre-screened in the mail room? Are instructions posted on the characteristics of suspicious mail and procedures for handling it?

√ Does the company use pre-employment screening techniques, including background checks and drug testing, to identify potentially troublesome candidates?

√ Does the company respond promptly to incidents of sexual harassment and internal conflicts?

√ Does the company have a crisis-management plan? If so, have the appropriate personnel been trained on the crisis-management plan?

√ Has the company instructed employees on security training procedures, stress management, sexual harassment, handling confrontations, drug abuse awareness, and warning signs for violent behavior?

If you can answer "yes" to most of these questions, you are probably in pretty good shape from a security standpoint. It's a good indication that your employer is doing their part to maintain the first line of defense in the workplace—protecting your well-being.

Any "no" answers are areas of security exposure. In that case, it's up to you to make your situation better. You can raise issues with the appropriate person. If you're going to point out a problem, it's a good idea to suggest a solution. Volunteer to help. That way you can be sure it gets done.

If your employer is not willing to participate in creating safer conditions for employees, there are other ways to motivate them. OSHA is cracking down on companies for failing to protect employees from violence. And the courts are increasingly holding employers accountable for the safety of employees.

You and Your Co-workers

Your role is simple in ensuring office safety. There are basically three things you need to do.

ABIDE BY THE RULES: Follow your employer's security procedures, whether it involves escorting visitors on the premises, locking doors behind you, or adhering to guidelines for hiring and firing personnel.

BE AWARE: You are the eyes and ears of your company. You'll be the first to know if something out of the ordinary occurs. It could be an unknown visitor wandering on the premises. Or it could be a co-worker who is exhibiting unusual behavior or is experiencing personal problems.

GET MANAGEMENT INVOLVED: Do not sit by passively if you sense that something is wrong. Take it to your supervisor. If your supervisor is the problem, take it to their boss.

Chapter 13

CHOOSING YOUR WEAPON

There are many fables and old wives' tales that describe the best weapon or household object that you can use to protect yourself. Many of them do not work. Remember from Chapter 3 that guns don't work because an intelligent person will hesitate before pulling the trigger. That split-second hesitation may cost you your life.

What Doesn't Work

KNIVES: If you carry an open knife in your purse or in your pocket, the first thing that's going to happen is that a hole will be cut—a hole in your purse or pocket. The second thing that's going to happen is that you are going to cut yourself. And pretty soon you take the hint and close that knife up and put it away somewhere. So knives don't work.

HAT PINS: Is a hat pin going to keep you safe? I don't think so. Now I don't know where people buy these things in the first place but they have them. Anyway, picture a woman standing waiting for a bus at nine-thirty at night. It's dark and deserted and some creep comes out of the woodwork to rob her. She pulls out her trusty hat pin and she waves it at him.

This guy can't see it so it doesn't frighten him. A hat pin will not go through heavy clothes or penetrate leather. And even if she does manage to stick him with it, it's only a pin! I mean, we're not talking massive tissue destruction here. So hat pins don't work either.

KEYS: Do you think holding your keys between your fingers will protect you? Most women—and many men—do not have the upper-body strength to deliver a good punch. Remember, the bad guys are very shrewd at picking who is and who isn't tough. They pick the most vulnerable one. They don't walk down the street and say, "Oh, there's a guy that looks like Sylvester Stallone, I think I'll pick on him."

It doesn't work that way. Chances are this guy is bigger and stronger and his arms are longer than yours. If those keys are spread out between each of your fingers, all this guy has to do is grab your hand and squeeze. Try it. It's very painful.

Now, if you're in big trouble and keys are all you've got, then here's what to do: Put one key between your first and second fingers and pop this guy as hard as you can. Aim for his eye. If you land a good blow, it should provide the short window of opportunity you need to break and run. That's what you do—you run.

WHISTLES: Simple, inexpensive, loud! Many recommend them. Well, I don't. Why? Because a whistle only works when you're blowing it, and if you're under attack you probably won't get the chance.

STUN GUNS: They are illegal in many states and can be very dangerous because you have to wait until he gets within arm's length to use them. Stun guns can look impressive when you trigger it and you see the sparks, but it is a contact weapon.

You have to be close. Within arm's length. Your arms, not his. He could knock it from your hand or kick it loose. And what if there are two bad guys? Add stun guns to the list of things that don't work.

What Does Work

As we've said, guns and knives, hat pins and keys, whistles and stun guns are either illegal or don't work—so what does? Screaming and using personal defense sprays and alarms work! (See Chapter 5 for specifics.)

DELBERT YEPKO

Here's an example of how pepper spray beat out a gun and saved some lives.

Delbert Yepko was sitting at home watching the eleven o'clock news when he heard a loud pounding at the front door. He had a gut feeling something was wrong. Even though Delbert had a loaded .38 in the house, he decided to grab his canister of pepper spray and went to the door. He turned the front light on and with his left hand took the latch off the door. As he cracked the door he saw a face and body and the whole door come at him.

He was totally shocked. But it didn't take him long to realize it was his step-daughter's ex-husband.

The ex-son-in-law barged into the middle of the living room and said, "I'm going to kill you." Delbert saw a wild look in his eyes and an object in his right hand. It was a pistol. At that moment, Delbert took action by firing off a burst of pepper spray into his face. The intruder immediately grabbed for his eyes and as he did, he fired the gun. Delbert kept the pepper spray on him and he fired again, wildly, with no aim. By now, the intruder had dropped to his knees and was doubled up on the floor. As he lay writhing in pain, Delbert backed up to the front door, knocked it open, ran out, and never looked back. He ran to a neighbor's house and called the police.

Delbert is convinced to this day that if he had taken his pistol to the front door, he would probably not be alive. Why? Because, despite the threat of murder from his ex-son-in-law, Delbert felt he would have tried to reason with him and may have hesitated in using the gun—like most intelligent people. Later that evening, Delbert was shocked to find out that his intruder had, just moments before banging on Delbert's door, killed Delbert's stepdaughter. For that murder, he was captured, tried, convicted, and sent to prison. It's a tragic story that could have been even worse. But thanks to his quick thinking, Delbert avoided becoming yet another victim of a twisted mind.

DIANNE ROSS

Dianne was walking home at night but she was paying attention. She was keeping a close watch on her shadow. When she moved directly under the streetlight, she couldn't see her shadow any longer, and it was at that point that somebody grabbed her from behind and dragged her into an alley. The guy then put Dianne on the ground. She was immobile due to a bout of arthritis as a young child. The arthritis affected her hands and knees, so she had no way to get up easily.

The bad guy looked around to see that the coast was clear and then he picked up Dianne and started running down the alley. She realized she was in real trouble and was afraid of being taken into a car. It was at that moment that she remembered what had been taught in her self-defense course.

With all the conviction she could muster, she decided that she would not be a victim. It was as if her instructor's face was right there saying, "What do you have? What have you got?" Then she realized she had teeth. Dianne reached over and bit him on the thumb as hard as she could. It startled him so much that he put her down and ran away.

I like to tell Dianne's story for a couple of reasons. This is a woman who cannot run and has limited use of her arms and legs. That greatly reduced her options in this situation. But she did have a plan. The self-defense course she took taught her about not being a victim. Dianne also took action. She learned that protecting herself was more than just punches and kicks—it was using her brain and not letting herself be taken anywhere.

Even though Dianne's plan was not perfect, it worked! For example, she could have acted sooner, or screamed "FIRE! FIRE! FIRE!" But her situation was unique, and any time you can get out of serious trouble alive and without serious harm you've done the right thing. If you find yourself in trouble and you miss that first opportunity to make your move, don't give up and don't give in. Stay as focused on getting away as you can. Look for another chance as soon as it presents itself.

Self-Defense

What if the bad guy keeps coming? Once he invades your personal space, don't be shy about protecting yourself. One method is to poke him in the eyes. But don't rationalize yourself out of it. Too many people think: It sounds too painful to poke someone in the eyes! or: That's too violent! Well, you can't be worried about that. Use all of your fingers, not just two. The other technique when it comes to the eyes is to jamb both thumbs deep into his eye sockets. That works also.

Some other things you can do to his head and face: pull his hair and use both hands. Give it a good yank and then get out of there. Or slap him with all you've got. When it's the face, I recommend a slap instead of a punch. It is much more effective and tougher to stop. Step across your body and follow through hard. A karate chop to the neck is effective but can be very difficult to execute.

If you go for the groin, that's where to use a punch. If you land a direct hit, he'll double over. You can also knee him in the groin, but a knee works just as well on his knee or his thigh. If he grabs you by the shoulders, twist out of his grasp and use your elbow to strike his chin. The foot stomp is another effective technique. The foot is a web of small bones, many of which are very fragile. So give him a good shot in the foot and you've got your shot to get out of there.

If he grabs you and you try to peel his hand off, that can be tough. He's probably too strong. But if you grab for his thumb and twist it back, that will work! Or if he has your wrist or arm, snap the wrist down and toward his thumb. Even the strongest bad guy will not be able to hold on.

If you get knocked down, swivel around on your backside and kick. Women do not have the upper-body strength to keep a grown male off them with the power in their arms. Neither do most men. But even a child has enough power in the legs to keep him off. Kick at him one leg at a time. A good shot to the knee or groin will disable him long enough for you to get away.

Dianne Ross obviously benefited from taking a self-defense course and I applaud her for that. I'm often asked about self-defense courses and my standard answer is this: In most situations, fleeing is going to be an option and, if it is, it is always your best option. Get your knees in the breeze and get out of there. Most people don't stay with self-defense courses long enough to achieve the level of skill needed to fight off some guy who is probably bigger and stronger.

Sometimes a little knowledge can be dangerous. It can lead to a false sense of security and put you in unnecessary danger. For example, if you are confronted by an armed robber, you might decide to fight this guy when all he wants is your purse. Well, that's not smart, and taking only a few classes in self-defense will not adequately prepare you for such a battle.

There are times, however, when fleeing is not an option because of a physical disability, as in Dianne Ross's case, or because of other circumstances. So if you have to fight this guy, then certainly some training will help.

Some self-defense courses advocate a lifestyle adjustment. They will teach you to be calm and cool in stress situations. They also will instruct you in how to channel your energy and focus your thoughts as well as defend yourself. These are good things to know. I believe that if you join a martial arts class for the overall and long-reaching results, they can be beneficial to your health as well as your safety.

I think the real value in these courses, if properly taught, is in teaching you to be aware of what's going on around you and carry yourself with an attitude.

Dawn Callan teaches a two-day workshop in the San Francisco area called "Awakening the Warrior Within." Her program is designed to teach people to protect themselves against violent attack and to identify areas in their lives where they feel disempowered and helpless, and helps them to regain their power. By the end of the workshop, Dawn expects her students to feel that they can absolutely handle themselves against a violent attack. She drives this home by integrating into the program a very realistic combat situation, where students face their worst fears and learn how to survive.

LOREE KILIAN

"There were about a dozen of us . . . men and women, all different ages. We spent a lot of time learning to use our hands, elbows, and legs to defend ourselves. But the big deal was actually testing ourselves in combat.

"Throughout the workshop, Dawn Callan reinforced one message over and over: That the class should enter into combat only if there was no other choice. If they see no other alternative, they must be 100 percent committed. So . . . there I was, all five feet, 105 pounds of me, ready to face my attacker.

"Actually, there were three of them and they took turns because it was very intense for us and them. Now these were very big guys . . . all over six feet tall and weighing in at more than two hundred pounds. We were in a large room with mirrors on the wall and a floor that was heavily padded. The attackers were also heavily padded and it was their job to pick the fight.

"But as soon as the attacker put his helmet on, it was our job to do anything we could to avoid being his victim. There were several rounds. And after each of the rounds, Dawn and the other instructors were right there to tell us what we were doing right and what we were doing wrong. They told us if we were being too timid. They told us if we were flailing with our arms instead of using a solid palm strike. And were we using our legs properly?

"One of the rounds of attack was an unprovoked assault and no holds were barred. We were instructed to do whatever it took to remain safe. Several others went ahead of me and the emotional level during and after was unbelievable. Many were in tears, both women and men. Then it was my turn. My heart was racing. The setup was this: I was walking to my car in a parking lot and this guy tries to abduct me. And, of course, I'm not about to let that happen. So I fought him with all I had and it was intense. Much more intense than I ever imagined it would be. All I can say is it was real . . . that weight, that strength, that power on top of your body. It's scary. But it was excellent training.

"I was so drained physically and emotionally at the end of the fight that about all I could say was 'Wow!' Because you just don't know what to do until you've been in that situation. You have no idea.

"As Dawn told us, we all come in knowing how to take care of ourselves but then it's put to sleep. And once those instincts are reawakened, they remain with us. I agree. I know I will never forget this experience, and I know because of it I'm much better prepared to take care of myself!"

Survival

The Tough Target attitude says, I have a plan. I am not going to get picked to play the game. And that's the right attitude. But sometimes an actual confrontation can not be prevented. When it happens, your primary goal is survival. The following factors can add to your Tough Target attitude and keep you on track.

MENTAL PREPAREDNESS: This means you know what you are going to do before the attack comes down. Have a plan! Make a firm resolution to do everything within reason to prepare for an assault. This may be frightening if you've never faced a violent situation, but you can diffuse much of that fear through preparation.

GOOD TACTICS: This takes mental preparedness to the next level. Tactics get down to specific actions. What exactly are you going to do in a particular situation? It's impossible to foresee every scenario but you can visualize most of them—attempts at carjacking, armed robbery, mugging, and home invasion. Put yourself in the shoes of the victims that you've read about. Think about what you would have done. Knowing what actions you will take in advance will make a difference.

SAFETY EQUIPMENT: Get expert advice in selecting your pepper spray, personal alarm, or other safety device. If you are in a confrontation and rely on emergency safety tools—but you can't make them work—what good are they? Training and preparation are critical because it's during that initial confrontation that the outcome of most encounters is decided. That's why I suggest using an inert training unit to become skilled with your pepper spray.

Fight or Flight

When you are attacked, your "fight-or-flight" mechanism kicks in. Literally hundreds of physiological and chemical reactions take place simultaneously during a period of intense stress. If you have training and you're prepared, reflex action takes over from conscious thought. That's your goal, because conscious thought means time—which you don't have. You need to react, not think about reacting.

The bad guy is counting on surprising you and if you surprise him, chances are you'll catch him off guard. And remember, defensive action should be an all-or-nothing response. Your capacity to perform at 100 percent is greatly enhanced if you are acting with reflex. And that means running as fast as you can, or striking as hard as you can, or yelling a command or "FIRE!" as loud as you can.

BOOK III

Chapter 14

SECURING YOUR HOME

Many communities today are virtually being held hostage by crime. What used to happen on the other side of town now takes place across the street or in your own home.

Burglaries are mostly a young person's crime. More and more such criminal activities are motivated by drugs and fast money. That makes the offenders dangerous and violent. They need cash, or property they can quickly convert to cash, and they don't care who stands in their way. This is different from the cat burglar who is a pro. He knows what he wants and is rarely violent. But he's only after the big businesses and the rich—and forget the rest. That's his motto. So most of us need to be concerned about the amateurs—the more violent criminals.

When it comes to home security, there are a number of simple, inexpensive things that you can do to reduce crime in our neighborhoods.

Home Security System

Here's the scoop on home security systems. There are several on the market that offer quality, affordable security for the average homeowner. And I stress average because these systems really are affordable, especially when you consider the benefits. Many insurance companies offer reduced premiums if your home is protected by a monitored alarm system.

Real estate brokers say that nothing will increase the value of your home more than a new kitchen. But a good alarm system is not far behind. You will benefit from the alarm system while you are living in the house and when you sell it.

As with any important purchase, give yourself some options. Call at least two or three reliable home security companies and compare products and services. Ask them for a free home security analysis and have them design a system that is right for you, your home, and your family.

Here's what you are looking for: a system that is electronically monitored twenty-four hours a day, every day of the year, with a staff of trained professionals monitoring the calls via advanced computer technology.

The components of the system itself will be similar among the top companies. However, some of these organizations will farm out the installation of the system to independent contractors. Others use their own employees. I suggest using the latter. That gives them control of the entire operation and results in a better chain of responsibility.

A standard system should include at a minimum: the keypad; door and window sensors to detect intruders; a master control unit to transmit information (with battery backup in the event of power failure); a siren to scare off intruders; and a yard sign and window decals to deter would-be burglars. The sign and window decals alone act as a deterrent to criminals. But don't purchase generic stickers at the local hardware store and think you'll be safe. Believe me, the bad guys know what's legit and what isn't.

The system should also include at least one emergency panic button that can be located wherever you want it in the home—like the master bedroom. Additional emergency buttons are usually optional but worth considering. The company you select should offer add-ons such as motion detectors, special glass-breakage detectors, and state-of-the-art smoke and heat detectors. That will protect you from fire or medical emergencies in addition to protection from burglaries. Consider all of these options and then settle on the best system you can afford.

Once the system is installed, it is important for every member of the family to understand how the system works and how to keep it activated. Usually it's a simple four-digit code that activates and deactivates the system. You want to purchase one that allows you to activate the entire system while you are away from home; then when you return, you can arm parts of the system to allow free movement by family members or pets while still protecting against intruders.

Of course, the bottom line is response time. In most systems, when a signal is received from your home security system it goes to the monitoring center, where it is received by a security professional. That person will quickly verify the alarm by calling the protected residence to confirm that there is an emergency and not a false alarm. If there is no answer, or if the person who answers does not give the correct code word, the police are immediately notified.

MADELINE AND BESSIE WILLIAMS

Madeline got home late from work one evening—it was around ten o'clock. She fixed her bedridden mother, Bessie, a light dinner, adjusted the television set in Bessie's bedroom, and went back to the kitchen to fix her own dinner. She brought it into the living room, where she sat down to watch the news. Little did she know that outside she had company—bad company.

Two guys in their early twenties were prowling around, ready to strike. They went to the back of the house, peered inside, and then went to work on the sliding-glass door. It took them only a couple of minutes to pry it open. They moved inside and crept cautiously into the kitchen. It was then that Madeline heard a noise. She got up from the sofa and, as she moved through the dining room toward the kitchen, she was confronted by these two guys.

She was scared half out of her wits and screamed. The first guy grabbed her, spun her around, and put his hand over her mouth. He told her to shut up and demanded money. The second guy ran down the hall and discovered Bessie. He told Madeline that they'd kill her mother if she didn't give them all the cash they had. Madeline realized she had left her purse in the car and told them so. The first guy tightened his stranglehold and continued with the threats as they ransacked the house looking for cash.

They told Madeline they would kill her if she called the police. They then grabbed the TV, VCR, and whatever else they could carry and they were gone. The whole incident lasted for five minutes.

Madeline, still in shock, regained her composure enough to hit the panic button on her home security alarm. Her file immediately popped on the computer screen at the headquarters of the home security company. A flashing light signaled an emergency. This is the actual emergency call:

SECURITY PROFESSIONAL: Hello. Do you have an emergency?

MADELINE: Yes, ma'am, we do. Please help us.

SECURITY PROFESSIONAL: Okay, calm down, calm down. The police are on the way. What's the nature of the emergency?

MADELINE: Well, there's two men. They broke into the house. I don't know how they got in, but they said they would kill my mother and me if we don't give them the money.

SECURITY PROFESSIONAL: Are the men still in the house?

MADELINE: No, no, they're gone now. But they took everything. And they said they were going to come back here and kill us.

SECURITY PROFESSIONAL: Okay. Okay. Just calm down, Mrs. Williams, everything will be all right now. My name is Rachel and I'll stay on the line with you until the police arrive. . . .

Madeline and Bessie were very lucky! These guys were out for drug money. They are violent criminals who will stop at nothing—even murder. Fortunately, Madeline and Bessie were not hurt.

But what's wrong with this picture? Madeline was smart to have a home security system installed. A hard-wired, monitored home security system is your best deterrent to burglaries and robberies. But you've got to keep it activated—especially when you're at home.

A hard-wired, monitored home security system is your best deterrent to burglaries and robberies. But you've got to keep it activated—especially when you're at home.

The Watchdog

If a monitored security system is your number one deterrent to crimes in the home, what is number two? It's a dog! Bad guys don't like dogs. Period.

It's important to keep in mind that if burglars wanted to make an honest living, they would get jobs. They don't. So it's important to make a break-in attempt as much work and worry for them as you possibly can.

That's why a dog is effective. Dogs have a keen sense of hearing and will respond to footsteps on the back porch or hallway long before you do. When they hear that noise they bark. Now the intruder hears this and he's got a decision to make. Because he doesn't know the dog's size or, more important, its temperament. So, chances are this guy will move on to the next home. It's easier and less worry. There's less chance of getting caught or having a bite taken out of his leg.

Here's how this works: Let's say there are two apartments right across the back porch from each other. If you went up the backstairs you would find that they have a common back porch. The door on the right is the same color as the door on the left. They've got the same type of door. The same kind of lock is on each door. The windows are exactly the same and the curtains are even the same color. These two apartments are identical in every way.

Except the woman on the left went to the pet store and bought a dog bowl—a BIG dog bowl! She wrote the word "Killer" on it and put it outside her door. Now, when the bad guy comes up the backstairs to burglarize one of these apartments, which one is he going to avoid? This can work with or without a dog. But the real thing is better.

Now, if you have a big dog bowl on the back porch, a dog inside, and your home has a monitored security system installed, your home is a Tough Target. And that's what you want.

Two women live in two identical apartments. The woman on the left bought a dog bowl—a BIG dog bowl—and wrote the word "Killer" on it. Which of these apartments is the bad guy not going to pick?

Selecting the Best Location

Let's look at some other ways to make your home a Tough Target. There's a saying in the real estate business that there are three important factors to consider when opening a retail operation—location, location, location. It also applies to the home.

Where you choose to live is one of the most important factors influencing risks of all types of crime. So, if you're looking for a new residence or planning a move down the road, keep that in mind. Pay as much attention to the crime situation as you do to schools, shopping, transportation, and other conveniences.

Talk to neighbors and the police in your prospective new neighborhood. Check to see how well structures are maintained. Ask about turnover. Areas with low turnover rates are usually also low-crime neighborhoods. So that does not mean it has to be an expensive upper-middle-class area to be stable and relatively crime-free.

Wherever you live, the more secure your home or apartment is, the more you will deter crime.

Safety on the Outside

The outside and surrounding areas are the first place the bad guys notice when choosing a crime target. A house that is neglected is a prime target, so keep hedges trimmed and be sure you have a clear view of all entrances. Keep your curtains closed at night and don't leave things like ladders out in the open. These guys are resourceful enough, you don't need to hand them your valuables on a silver platter! When you leave, put the radio on and be sure there are lights on at night.

WINDOWS: There's a simple, inexpensive way to make your windows secure. A few nails, a hand drill, and five minutes of your time per window is all it takes. Here's what you do: Close the window—you'll notice that the upper frame of the bottom window and the lower frame of the upper window meet in the middle. Drill one hole in each corner. The hole should go completely through the inner frame and halfway through the outer frame.

Drill these holes at a slight downward angle. Insert a nail with a smaller diameter than the hole and trim the pointed end off so that the nail head fits flush with the wooden frame. With nails inserted through both window frames, no amount of pressure from the outside will open the window—even if the lock has been broken. To open the window from the inside, simply pull out the nails.

LOCKS: Despite the number of second-story cat burglars seen on television, eighty percent of all burglars gain entrance the old-fashioned way: through the front door. And they don't do it by picking locks. They just kick in the door.

I'm not saying that locks aren't important. They are. Unfortunately, many new home builders install key-in-knob locks because they are inexpensive and easy to install. These should be considered privacy locks only, not security locks. The door can be locked without keys and that makes it convenient for the homeowner. The bad guys have a field day with this because it's easy for them to open.

The key-in-knob is fine if it uses a tapered free-spinning cylinder guard and a deadbolt lock to supplement it. Again, because of the cost, most deadbolts are made of brass, an easy metal to cut. Choose a deadbolt that is at least one-inch long and made of hardened steel.

Not many burglars walk around with a tool kit. Which brings us back to the most popular form of illegal entry into the home: the jump kick! It's fast and requires no tools or special skills.

When the door flies open from the kick it's most often not the door or lock that gives, it's the strike plate—a standard strike plate is a thin piece of metal that is attached to a door frame by small screws and it can be easily ripped out of the wood with a couple of hard kicks. So no matter how good the lock, if the strike plate is weak, the lock is weak. A reinforced, high-security strike box, installed with long screws, will strengthen your deadbolt, and that's what you want. Consult with a professional locksmith for advice on the best lock/strike box combination for you.

GARAGE: What about garages attached to the house? Well, the garage should be treated like any other entrance and be secure. The door should be strong and is best secured by an electronic garage-door opener. Make sure the garage door leading into the home is as strong as the front and back doors, and keep it locked.

DOORS: Great hardware is not much good unless the door itself is strong. That strength depends on material and construction. Heavy steel doors at least 1 3/4-inches thick with a steel frame or Calamine doors (metal wrapped over solid-core wood), are your best bet.

I suggest staying away from doors that have glass inserts. The glass can be easily broken and, unless it is frosted or tinted, it allows thieves to see into your home. Peepholes are good, however.

Many homes and apartments have sliding-glass doors and they can be problems. Why? Because they're designed with a small lock that can be easily forced open. That's how the bad guys got into Madeline and Bessie's home. Also, their aluminum frames can be bent and the doors lifted off their tracks.

To reinforce sliding-glass doors, I suggest having a stronger lock installed. Also, many people wedge a broomstick in the door. The bad guy with a coathanger can defeat that. A pipe with an open end laid in the track is not much better. But these things only keep the door from sliding. They will not prevent the door from being lifted off its track.

Locks installed on the top of these doors are hard to reach and will not be used routinely. I suggest purchasing an adjustable safety bar with an anti-lift feature. There are several good safety bars on the market and, once again, a professional locksmith can advise you on which one to choose.

But what good is any of this stuff if you don't keep your door locked? This may sound like a no-brainer, but I am constantly amazed at how many people walk out their front door without locking it. And more important—keep the doors locked when you are home. If you are gone when they break into your home, all they get is your stuff. But if your family is home the risk and danger go up tremendously.

I've seen too many cases where people have been upstairs or out in the backyard while an intruder has snuck in, grabbed the TV and other valuables, and was gone before anyone noticed.

Lighting

There is no better value or benefit than proper lighting for keeping your home safe—if you know how to use it.

Since a majority of crimes occur at night, good lighting not only reduces your risk of being burglarized, it also allows you to find your keys and get inside quickly. That makes you less vulnerable if some guy is hiding in the bushes waiting to rob you.

All of your exterior doors, and as many windows as practical, should be lit at night, as well as the house numbers, which will make them readable in case of a fire, police, or medical emergency. I recommend automatic lighting controls. These are motion control devices that automatically turn on lights whenever someone nears the doors or enters the driveway.

Be sure to install lighting devices out of easy reach and protect them from the elements by encasing them in weather-resistant housings.

What about indoor lighting? Stairs, hallways, bathrooms, basements, and other areas can be made safer and more secure with good lighting. Automatic lighting controls that light the area whenever someone walks near it work well. And night-lights work also. They don't use much electricity and they do the job.

When you plan to be away at night, close the blinds and curtains and use timers to turn on lights in a couple of rooms at least—consider the living room and a bedroom.

Many home invaders pick houses on a vulnerability scale and because they know what's inside. So don't keep lots of cash or expensive jewelry in the house. And never open the door for someone you don't know.

Break-ins

If you have left home and return to something suspicious—like an open door or window or items out of place—walk right back out the door and go to a neighbor's to call police. In most cases, your first reaction is to rush around to check on damage or theft, but that's not smart. You may be putting yourself at risk of confronting an armed burglar.

If you return home to something suspicious—like an open door or window or items out of place—walk right back out the door and go to a neighbor's to call police.

VICKI MARTIN

Unfortunately, Vicki Martin lost more than just valuables.

Vicki Martin, age twenty-five, was on the fast track. She graduated at the top of her class from Roosevelt University and immediately landed a job as an accountant with a large company located in downtown Chicago. In three short years she was on her way to becoming the head of her department. From there to the executive suite. Everybody agreed Vicki was a smart professional, very effective and very efficient—traits she carried over into her personal life.

Vicki lived in a small, one-bedroom, first-floor apartment on the north side of the city. It was a convenient location, just a short walk from the El station where she boarded a train that stopped just a half-block from her office building. Her daily routine rarely varied. Every morning at seven-thirty she put Max, her beagle, out in the yard while she ate breakfast, then locked him back in the apartment when she left for work at eight.

She walked out the back door of her apartment, through the backyard, and down the alley to the El stop. She did this because it was shorter—effective and efficient—and took less time. It saved her about three minutes. In the evening she would get off the six-thirty train, take the same route through the alley to her back door, and let Max out to do his business.

She would leave the back door open. She would then change her clothes and begin to make dinner. When she heard Max come back in, she would close and lock the door. No time lost. Effective and efficient.

Vicki didn't know she was being watched. One night the bad guy made his move. He saw Vicki as she left the train station and followed her through the alley to her back door. While the dog was out in the yard and the back door was open, he slipped into the kitchen.

I know she confronted him on the rear porch because the shade was torn off. The dog was stabbed in the kitchen with a knife that the perpetrator picked up off the counter. He chased Vicki into the dining room, where he ripped off her blouse. All four buttons were found in the dining room within an area of about thirty-six inches. We found her in the living room, laying over a hassock. She had been fatally stabbed 107 times. Max did survive and was adopted by another family.

Here's what we can learn from her story:
• When you're walking at night, take the extra time to walk into or toward the light. Not away from it. Except in the summertime, it's usually dark after work. Walking alone anytime through the alley is not smart. Walking at night is even less smart.

- Do not leave the back door open. Even a screen door, as frail as it is, will give you more warning and protection than an open door.
- If someone is trying to come through a secure, locked door—even a screen door—you should have enough time to run out, get into the bedroom, lock the door, and call 911. Once you have 911 on the phone do not hang up. Stay on the line with the dispatcher until the police arrive. This is the best way. The dispatcher can keep you calm and tell you what to do; and you can tell the dispatcher what is happening and how many bad guys are there.

Vicki's case was tragic, but with a little forethought and some simple precautions, Vicki Martin's murder could have been prevented.

Knock, Knock, Who's There?

If there is a stranger at your door and the person says he's with a utility company, ask to see his ID. This is where the peephole comes in handy. If you're suspicious, say you are calling the utility company to check it out. And don't be fooled by uniforms. They are easy to obtain.

Also, watch out for scams. Here's one that is often used. It goes like this: The goof comes to your door and says his car has broken down and asks to use the phone to call for a tow truck. You look out the window and sure enough, there's a car outside with the hood up. What do you do? Offer to make the call for him. But do not let him inside!

Creating a Safe Room

Most burglars are not looking for confrontation. They are looking for an unoccupied residence. They want to get in, steal whatever they can, and get out as quickly as possible. Most of these guys are not interested in a showdown.

But let's say you're home alone, in bed, and you hear a noise downstairs. The best defense once an intruder is inside is to have a "safe room" in your home. That could—and probably should—be the master bedroom.

The door to the safe room should be solid, with a steel frame, and equipped with a deadbolt lock. Inside should be a cellular phone, a three-ounce canister of pepper spray, and if you have a monitored alarm system, a panic button.

If you are in your safe room and you hear someone in your home, jump out of bed, close the door, and slide that deadbolt into place. If you have an alarm system, hit the panic button. (He shouldn't be in there in the first place if the system is armed and working, but maybe he's circumvented it somehow.) Get to your phone and call 911. If the line is dead use the cell phone. When you reach the police, tell them the situation and then stay on the line with the dispatcher. This dispatcher will ask questions and relay this information to the responding units. The dispatcher will also tell you what to do.

If, at this point, the bad guy is still rummaging around downstairs—don't interrupt him. You've got the police on the way and he'll have some unwanted visitors shortly. You want to avoid any confrontation with this guy if you can. Remember, he's probably there to steal your valuables and will only become violent if he feels threatened.

If you hear him at your door or if he's trying to get through that door, then the situation changes. Now, you're in real danger.

Yell, "Bobby, get the shotgun!" Even if there is no Bobby! Let him know you've called the police and, if you feel it's necessary, throw a lamp or chair through the window. Scream, "FIRE! FIRE! FIRE!" That will get the neighbors involved.

Once you've done all this, chances are this guy is going to leave in a hurry. He knows you are tough and he also knows the police are on their way. But if he still persists, and he gets through that door, have your pepper spray in hand. If you nail him with that spray, he'll go down and you'll have your chance to get out of there. And that's what you do. Get out of there!

Handling House Keys

Do not hide house keys under doormats, in planters, or in mailboxes. Those are the first places the bad guys look. If your keys are lost or stolen, or you have just moved into a new home or apartment, have the locks changed. It's also a good idea to do a videotape audit of your home to record valuables. In case the bad guys do get in, this provides proof to the insurance company and helps the police. Engraving your driver's license number on valuables is another smart thing to do.

Women Who Live Alone

If you are a woman living alone, don't put your first and last name on the mailbox or in the phone directory. Use only the first initial of your first name. Have a male relative or friend put his voice on your answering machine and do not leave messages on the machine saying you are out of town.

Get Involved

Get involved in a neighborhood watch program. Or if there is no program in your neighborhood, help get one started.

The safest neighborhoods are those where people look out for one another. The National Crime Prevention Council reports that in many communities crime has been reduced by more than half when these programs are put in place.

Most police departments provide information on organizing and implementing crime-watch programs. They will also offer ongoing support by providing a continuing liaison to help with crime-related problems that develop. There is strength in numbers, and these programs work because they are easy to set up and maintain and they don't require a lot of time from any one individual or family.

Even if you consider yourself a loner, at least get to know a couple of your neighbors. If you live in an apartment complex or condo building, attend tenant or association meetings. Whatever your situation, get involved. Don't expect the other guy to do it. Remember to help each other out!

Chapter 15

SAFEGUARDING YOUR CAR

For most people the purchase of a motor vehicle is the second-largest investment made. Anything of value is a potential target for the bad guys. According to the National Insurance Crime Bureau (NICB), over 1.5 million vehicles were reported stolen in 1994—the equivalent of one theft every twenty seconds.

Car theft is the most costly property crime in the United States, with an estimated cost of $7.6 billion. Two-thirds of the thefts occur at night. Sixty-two percent of the vehicles stolen in 1994 were recovered, although most of those were either stripped or vandalized. Those not recovered were: shipped overseas or driven across U.S. borders; surgically stripped by chop shops and resold as parts; retagged and resold to unsuspecting consumers; and hidden or destroyed by the owner to collect insurance money.

Keep in mind that older vehicles are stolen as frequently as newer ones. The parts on older cars grow more valuable as cars age. Most chop shop operators make two to four times a vehicle's actual value by selling its parts separately. And unlike rape and stalking statistics—where actual incidents are difficult to assess—there is no problem with statistics on vehicle-related crimes. If your car is stolen, you report it. One, you want it back. And two, if you don't get it back, you need to have the police report to take to your insurance company. So these statistics are accurate.

What is the profile of the car thief? There is none. Like most criminals, car thieves come in all shapes and sizes. Many are juveniles who get involved in car theft rings because the risk of being caught is low and if they are caught, they often get off with a warning and then go right back on the streets.

To appreciate the extent of the problem, it's a good idea to look at the market for stolen cars and how that market is exploited.

Many cars are stolen just for the parts. It's big business to steal a car and take it to a chop shop where it is stripped down. And it happens fast! A skilled chop shop operator can surgically strip a car in under thirty minutes.

While theft of an expensive luxury car may be the big prize, car thieves don't discriminate. You can be just as vulnerable in a Chevy as in a Lexus.

The most commonly stolen vehicle parts and contents include stereos, cellular phones, and wheels. Increasingly, auto thieves are targeting vehicles for their fancy parts or accessories. The more sophisticated the accessory, the more sophisticated the thief. Air bags are the latest item of choice. They can be easily removed, they are portable, and they can be installed as new by dishonest repair shops who charge the victim or the victim's insurance carrier full price for the replacement.

Hundreds of thousands of stolen U.S. vehicles are shipped overseas or driven across U.S. borders every year. In some schemes, the stolen cars are fitted with new Vehicle Identification Numbers—a VIN is a serial number used to differentiate similar makes and models—markings, and license plates. They are taken to ports, crated, and sealed in intentionally mislabeled containers and shipped overseas.

Switching VINs is a technique of increasing popularity with car thieves. Like social security numbers, every vehicle has a different VIN. It's located on the dashboard and is visible through the windshield. Law enforcement agencies use VINs to determine if a vehicle has an active theft record. By switching the VIN on a stolen vehicle, the thieves have just created an excellent disguise. They will then try to resell the stolen car to an unsuspecting customer.

When it comes to vehicle-related security and safety, the rules that apply to your person and to your home apply here as well: The Tough Target does not get picked! Let's say there are two identical cars parked on the street. One of these cars has packages on the backseat, a cellular phone in the front seat, an unlocked door, and the keys dangling from the ignition. The other car has no packages, no cellular phone, locked doors, no keys, and a small, blinking red light inside that signals a car alarm.

Well, this is easy. You're the bad guy and you are out to steal a car. Which one of these two cars are you going to pick? Car number one might as well put a neon sign on top saying: "Steal me." Sound too easy? Not when you consider that of all the vehicles that are stolen each year, 80 percent are unlocked and nearly 20 percent had keys in the ignition.

Case in point: One winter morning, a driver of a Mercedes pulls up in front of a bagel store and goes into the store, leaving his keys in the ignition. It was very cold outside and very warm inside, so the floor-to-ceiling windows were steamed up. Everything outside was shrouded in fog and barely visible. Now the bagel shop is a popular place and there is often a line. On this particular morning, it was about eight deep. He waited in line, got his bagels, and left. Fortunately for the Mercedes guy, his car was still there. Had a car thief been hanging out there that morning, he could have been in this guy's car and out of that parking lot in a minute—with a nice new Mercedes as his prize! And he could have done it all virtually unnoticed, certainly before the owner of that car could have responded.

How often have you done the very same thing? Jumped out of your car, left it running to dash inside a store or to drop off your dry cleaning or pay for your gasoline. Seems innocent enough, yet it is because of these very kinds of situations that the statistics on car thefts have gone through the roof.

So what do you do? It's simple. When you leave your car do this: Always take the keys, lock the doors, make sure there are no valuables in sight, and if you have a purse or briefcase, take it with you. As basic as these precautions are, most car thefts would be eliminated if these steps were followed.

Always park in a safe area, and when you leave your car, take the keys, lock the doors, make sure there are no valuables in sight.

Combating Carjackers

There are several different carjacking scenarios. Carjackers attack motorists at traffic lights, gas stations, parking lots, fast-food drive-throughs, and in other areas where they are stopped or exiting their vehicles. Increasingly, carjacking gangs employ the "bump and run" technique. They bump the car of an unsuspecting driver and, when the driver gets out to check the damage, the thieves forcibly take the car.

It's also the reason why another vehicle-related crime has soared in recent years. The police call it armed robbery. The media call it carjacking. Call it whatever you want, but it's a crime that was virtually unheard of ten years ago. You can prevent this easily by locking your doors when you get in the car. Simple!

Most carjackings occur between eight and eleven P.M., more often on weekends than during the week. The most active month is December, when over 25 percent of carjackings take place. Over 90 percent of carjackings take place in fifteen metropolitan areas.

Carjacking is a crime which—like car theft—can be deterred by following these simple steps: When you get in your car, lock the doors immediately. Make sure the windows are rolled up. That's it. If you do these things, you are a tougher target than the person driving behind you with the windows down and the doors unlocked.

When you get in your car, lock the doors immediately and make sure the windows are rolled up.

I've performed experiments with news crews to see how safe people are inside their cars. I tell you, they'd be a lot safer if they followed these two simple rules. Case in point: A news crew and I set up at Ontario Street and Wabash Avenue in Chicago; at this point Ontario is a one-way street with five lanes across. It is a feeder street to one of our expressways.

It was around four in the afternoon and the evening rush hour had just begun. The Ontario streetlight turned red and the traffic stopped. I walked out into the traffic with the cameraman. We approached the first car in the middle lane. I walked up to the driver's door and pulled the door handle. My goal was to see if I could open the driver's door. I did this experiment fifteen times. Twice the door was locked. If you lock your doors every time, you're driving safer than 90 percent of the population.

I performed this experiment another time for a news magazine show and the results were similar. Now, when I speak to groups, I always pose this question: How many people in the audience lock their car doors once they get inside? A majority of hands go up. Every time. Well, my little exercise is certainly not statistically valid but I believe it's pretty close to being valid. It tells me there is a big discrepancy between what people say they do and what they really do.

DONNA DEHART

Donna and her nine-month-old daughter, Alyssa, were having a fun day doing their weekly shopping. They left the store at noon because a raging snowstorm was about to start and Donna wanted to get home.

She'd parked in the middle of the parking lot and there were cars and people all around. Donna checked to see if there was anyone lurking around her car but she didn't see anyone suspicious.

The first thing she did was put Alyssa in her car seat in the back. Then she went around and put their packages on the seat next to her. Donna put the stroller in the trunk and then got into the car. She was just closing the door when she felt something pull on it. She turned and there was this big man with a beard next to her and he had a gun. He said to Donna, "Move over or I'll shoot you right here."

Donna noticed that the man didn't smell of alcohol or appear to be on drugs. She knew he had rape or murder on his mind and knew she had to get out of that car to save herself and her daughter. So she faked him out. She pretended that she was going along with him, slid across the front seat, grabbed at the passenger door, and when the door flew open she rolled out. Then Donna started to scream bloody murder.

Her only mistake was that she didn't get out of the line of fire. Because that's when she was shot. She didn't feel a lot of pain—but there was a lot of blood. Donna thought he was going to try to run her over, but with the screaming and the gunshot noise, they were attracting a lot of attention. The guy took off in the car with Alyssa still in the backseat.

And somehow as all this was going on, Donna was remembering two carjackings that had been on the news. One of them was a lady in a minivan. They had found her body in a ditch but the child had been left unharmed, dropped off at a day care center. The other involved a woman in a BMW. When she tried to get her child out of the car seat, they dragged her to death.

So Donna knew her chances were best if she could get some help to track the car. She managed to get up and chased the car across the parking lot, still screaming as loud as she could. All she could think about was saving her baby.

Donna ran up to a couple in a car and told them what had happened and convinced them to help. They started following the guy and then Donna spotted a police car, so she jumped out and told the officer what had happened and that's when the search began.

The police officer got on the radio right away and let the dispatcher know the description of the car and the direction in which it was headed. Fortunately, there was a lot of citizen involvement. Someone saw the carjacker abandon the car and told police, who were able to track his footsteps in the snow. They found the carjacker hiding out at the home of his girlfriend.

Donna and Alyssa both were safe. Some women would say they would have stayed with their baby. But Donna thought of the advice they give on the airlines when you need to use the oxygen mask. You have to take care of yourself first so you can then take care of your baby. Donna knew that she needed to stay alive so she could save her child.

Donna DeHart had only split seconds to make up her mind. And remember, she was looking down the barrel of a gun! So, like Donna, you need to know what you're going to do before the crime comes down. That's got to be part of your plan. So is attracting attention. And other people got involved and helped each other out.

PAMELA BASU

There is perhaps no more tragic example of this than the story of Pamela Basu. Ironically, Pamela lived in a Maryland town called Savage, a name that not only set the scene but ominously fit the profile of the crime.

The day began like any other day, except this was Sarina's, Pamela's twenty-two-month-old daughter's, first day of preschool. Pamela dressed her in a new outfit and together they left their townhome at about eight-thirty A.M. After strapping her daughter in the car seat of her BMW, Pamela proceeded to drive to the end of the parking lot of the complex, where she stopped at the stop sign.

Pamela was suddenly confronted by two unarmed men. They opened the front door and yanked her from the car. Pamela scrambled to gain her balance and, fearing for her daughter, managed to open the back door to get to Sarina. The two guys, meanwhile, jumped in the front seat and the one behind the wheel started to drive away. Pamela's left arm became entangled in the car seat and she was dragged in tow.

A neighbor described the horror she witnessed: "Pamela looked like one of those dummies they stuff up for Halloween. The BMW went about 1,000 feet and stopped. The driver got out, stepped over Pamela, walked around the car, and opened the right rear door. He grabbed the baby, lifted her from the car seat, and just tossed her in the road. And then he sped off."

The neighbor ran to help Sarina and then called the police. Pamela was still a prisoner of the car seat and was dragged mercilessly for more than a mile. The police responded quickly to the neighbor's call and were soon in hot pursuit of the stolen car. The driver lost control shortly after the chase began and crashed into a fence.

The bad guys abandoned the vehicle and made a dash for freedom while Pamela lay in a bloody heap, still hanging from the car. She had been ripped to shreds.

Rodney Eugene Solomon and Bernard Eric Miller, twenty-six and seventeen respectively, were apprehended immediately. They later told police they had gone in search of a car when their own vehicle ran out of gas on the nearby expressway. Several months later they were brought to trial and convicted of robbery, kidnapping, and murder. Pamela Basu did not survive the ordeal.

Pamela's case turned out to be the first of a string of carjackings in and around Washington, D.C., during the fall of 1992. Her death—and the cold, vicious manner in which it was carried out—made national headlines and became a rallying cry for the carjacking issue. This helped provide the necessary impetus to pass a bill which makes carjacking a federal crime. The law also requires automobile manufacturers to mark thirteen different car parts with ID numbers to help discourage the sale of stolen parts.

Pamela Basu felt comfortable and safe. How many times have you been in those very same circumstances? How many times have you jumped into your car and driven away with the car doors unlocked?

Unfortunately for Pamela, it cost her her life. Had the doors been locked, these guys would never have gotten into that vehicle unless she let them in.

This case made the national news because it was so senseless and so tragic. But it certainly is not an isolated case. These carjacking crimes are happening every day, to ordinary people. And in no way are vehicle thefts confined to large cities. Big increases are showing up in small and mid-sized cities as well.

If your car is in the parking lot of a mall or a supermarket, there is a very narrow window of opportunity open to the bad guy if he targets you and your vehicle.

He can't get you when you are in the store and he can't get you when you are driving away. He can only get you when you're at the car. But this narrow window expands a lot when you have packages, or a small child, or both. In fact, you are most vulnerable when your head is in the car as you try to deal with those packages or that child. Here's how to deal with parking lots:

- Many supermarkets have employees assigned specifically to help customers in these situations. Have that employee escort you to your car. It costs you a buck or two for a tip, but you get some help and you also stay safe.

- Remember, the bad guy goes for the easy target, and if there are two of you he's going to take a pass. He'll wait for the next one. But if you are alone, be aware of your surroundings. Start looking when you are about thirty feet away from the car. Is there anyone suspicious lurking about? If there is, go right back to the store and tell the manager. As you approach the car, look around and inside the vehicle. And have your keys in hand. This accomplishes two things: One, you get into your car right away rather than standing around fumbling for those keys; and two, you have easy access to the pepper spray hanging from your key ring (I hope you have one of these units by now). That alone makes you a tougher target!

As you approach the car, look underneath and inside the vehicle.
Have your keys and pepper spray in hand.

When you get to your car here's what to do:

• Put the packages in the trunk.

• Put the child in the car seat, but don't worry about buckling up the child at this point. Just get in the car, lock the doors, and start the engine. Then, reach over and strap the child in the car seat.

   The reason that you do it this way is to ensure that you and the child stay together as a unit. If you are interrupted while loading the groceries, and he takes the car, you still have the child. But if you put the child in first and then open the trunk and are loading groceries when he approaches, he has the car and the child.

• Bending into a car trunk to load groceries is a very vulnerable position. But you can minimize the danger. At an auto supply store buy two convex mirrors, one about one inch in diameter and the other about three inches. Open the trunk of your car, lean in the way you would if you were loading groceries or your luggage. Mount the larger mirror on the inside of the trunk lid or at the back of the trunk. That way, you'll be able to see anybody approaching. Use it like a rear-view mirror when you are loading and you won't be surprised.

   Take the smaller mirror and attach it to the driver's side rearview mirror. This will provide coverage of the blind spot to the driver's left rear while in traffic, and also reveal anybody approaching the car from that angle while you are stopped at a red light.

   Pay attention to the sounds around you. If a car stops near you or in the next aisle, look up and see what is going on and who is approaching. The more warning you have, the more time you have to react.

• Once you're safely in the car, loaded and locked, you're on your way. Now if a bad guy tries to open the car door, drive away. Quickly! Hit the gas and go. It's very unlikely he will shoot because that will only draw attention to himself. And he has a lousy angle on the driver. It's a tough shot to begin with and it only gets worse the farther away you are.

But what if some guy does come out of nowhere? What if he has a weapon and he gets to you before that door is locked? If he wants your vehicle and that's all he wants, your choice is simple. Let him have it! Get out of the car. Do not argue. Do not plead or beg. And do not fight! No car is worth fighting for and they surely are not worth dying for. Just get out. He's got your car but you are out of danger.

Trick Keys

Let's say you're in a situation similar to Donna's: a guy with a gun tells you to move over and to stay in the car. Learn from Donna—she kept her wits about her. She played it smart. She knew she had to save herself if she had any chance of saving her baby. So she made her move right away.

Donna dove out of the passenger side of the car and, despite being shot, that action probably saved her life. Here's what I recommend if this guy attacks you when you have your child in the car and he demands the car and you.

When the bad guy makes his demand, grab the car keys and say, "Take the keys, take the car, I'm taking my baby." Then toss the keys out the window—preferably so they land under another car. Chances are, he'll tell you to stay put and go for the keys.

When he does go for the keys, pull your child over the seat toward you and get out of the car. Do not run around the car to the other side to get the child. It takes too much time—what if the child's door is locked? Then you're in trouble. Pull the child over the seat and get out! And do not go back in. It's like a burning building—once you're out, you can't go back in.

There is something else you can do. Take a set of keys from that old car you traded in three years ago—and keep them in the car. Hang them from the flasher knob on your steering wheel column or keep them in your ashtray. If you are confronted, throw the old set of keys.

When he goes for the keys, lock your door. Then start your engine and drive away. Now, this guy has a dilemma. He thought the keys to your car were lying on the ground. So he had to crawl partially under the other car to get them. Now he sees you drive away and he has no chance of getting the car. Do you know how angry and frustrated he will be when you drive away?

That's how angry and frustrated you are when the bad guy has the plan. But it's nice to turn the tables on these guys. And you don't have to spend a lot of money to do that. But you do have to be prepared. You have to have a plan. If he uses the weapon as you are driving away, he will attract attention to himself but he won't be in the car. My guess is that he'll put the weapon back under his coat and wait for someone else.

Donna DeHart made her move immediately and it probably saved her life. Yes, she did take a bullet, but the bullet wound healed. What was the likely alternative?

Well, if this guy had taken her into that car, she'd have been on a one-way trip—and so would her baby.

The Smash and Grab

There's another car-related crime that is never out of style with the bad guys. It's what we call the smash and grab. You can check this one out yourself. Just stand on any busy street corner and watch for cars with only one driver.

When the cars stop, look to see what's on the passenger-side seat. If it's a woman driving, there is probably a purse. If it's a man, it might be a briefcase. But whatever it is, it's sitting there right out in the open and that makes it an easy target.

The smash and grab is a crime of opportunity, and here's how it comes down. The bad guy hangs out on the corner and when he sees his mark, he strikes. All it takes is a ball bearing the size of a pea and a decent throwing arm. When that ball bearing hits the glass, the glass shatters. As you cover your face in shock, his hand is inside the car, he pulls out the purse, and he's gone. And there's no way you are going to catch this thirteen-year-old kid in sneakers.

How long does all this take? About two seconds! That's it. So now you've got a car with a broken window, your purse is missing, and this kid knows where you live because your ID is probably inside the purse. Bad scene.

There's a simple solution to this. The purse or briefcase belongs on the floor of the car. That's all it takes. My first choice for location? Under the knees. My second choice? Up under the dash on the passenger side. In either case it's out of sight, and if it's out of sight he's not going to try for it. He'll wait for the next one.

The purse or briefcase belongs on the floor of the car—under your knees, or up under the dash. If the bad guy can't see it, he won't try for it.

There's one more place for your purse and that's in the trunk of the car. (And that's where the lady who's ahead of me in the toll booth line usually has hers!)

Let's look at another situation. You're on the expressway and suddenly someone pulls up beside you as you're driving and motions you over. A flat tire, maybe? Maybe not.

EILEEN WELDON

Eileen was driving on the expressway at ten o'clock in the morning. She was on her way to the store. She looked over and a truck driver had pulled up alongside her and he was motioning to her as if something was wrong with the car. She pulled over and he pulled up behind her.

But Eileen knew that she should keep the windows up and the doors locked. And she was not going to get out of the car.

The truck driver told her that her rear tire looked flat. He asked her for a tire iron. Eileen said she didn't have one and drove away. She was worried that her tire might fall off, so she drove away very slowly. She got off the expressway immediately and went straight to a service station. The attendant told Eileen that all the tires were fine and that she had no problems.

Eileen did the right thing. Who knows what that truck driver had in mind! If she had gotten out of her car and gone to the trunk to find her tire iron, what could have happened? She would have been alone with this guy and his truck was blocking the view of other drivers passing by. She would have been in big trouble.

The Side of the Road

What should you do if you have a flat and need to pull over to the side of the road? If someone signals to you that you have a flat and pulls over behind you, don't get out of the car! Ask the person to call the police on their CB or use their cellular phone. Do not, under any circumstances, get out of the car. And what if there's car trouble and you're alone out there? Same rule applies. Stay with the car. I don't want you walking down that highway alone or accepting a ride with a stranger.

This is where your cellular phone is invaluable. Remember, it's like a spare tire. You hope you never need it, but it's there if you do. So carry a cellular phone and call for help . . . and know the emergency number in your area.

If you don't have a cellular phone, put a sign in the back window that says: HELP! CALL POLICE! Even if you don't have a cellular phone, someone passing by will have one and that person will call the police for you. And if some helpful guy stops? Same thing. Just ask him to call the police. If you think he's suspicious, tell him someone just stopped before he did and the police are on the way. Repeat: Do not get out of the car!

Now, there's a variation on this situation and it's called the bump. It's not likely to happen on the expressway because the speeds are too high. It does happen, however, at stop signs and stoplights, and other places where speeds are low.

The Bump

It goes like this: You're driving in a quiet, rather secluded area. You may be lost and you're looking around to get your bearings. Suddenly you get bumped from behind. An innocent fender bender? Maybe. But maybe not. Why? Because these situations can quickly escalate into dangerous, sometimes deadly, encounters.

That's exactly what happened to Barbara Meller-Jensen, age thirty-nine, a visitor from Berlin, Germany. She arrived in Miami in April 1993 with her mother and two children in tow for what was supposed to be two weeks of sun, sand, and sightseeing. Her husband, Christian, remained home to work on his thesis.

BARBARA MELLER-JENSEN

It was around eight P.M. when the family boarded a courtesy bus at Miami International Airport to pick up a rental car. They piled their luggage into the trunk of the vehicle and headed for Miami Beach.

About five miles from the airport, apparently lost, she drove into a world far from the slick art-deco neighborhoods of South Beach. Just off Interstate 95, is an area in which tropical nights hold no magic, only poverty and danger. There, Meller-Jensen turned onto a relatively quiet street near an elementary school. Suddenly her car was hit from behind. She got out to check the damage and was immediately overcome by two men from the other car. They demanded her purse.

Then, as her mother and two children, ages six and two, watched in horror, the men grabbed her purse, beat her with their fists, and knocked her to the ground.

The thieves ran back to their car, and as they drove away, their tires rolled over Meller-Jensen's head. She was pronounced dead shortly after arrival at the hospital. Her wallet had fallen out of her purse during the scuffle and the killers got absolutely nothing.

Less than two days later, the two guys were arrested in an unrelated purse-snatching incident. When the purse was returned, its owner found an address label inside with Meller-Jensen's name on it. The cold-blooded killers went down formurder.

Meller-Jensen's violent and tragic death became headline news both nationally and internationally. The media coverage, in part at least, was instrumental in moving Miami—and the state of Florida—to implement a series of programs to help ensure the safety of tourists. It also prompted rental car companies to do the same thing. I'll talk more about rental cars in the chapter on travel.

For now, let's look at these bump and run situations. What do you do? Make sure your doors are locked and your windows are up. And do not get out of the car! Instead, turn on your emergency flashers and drive to a place where you feel safe.

If you can't move for some reason, and the other driver approaches your car, roll down the window a crack. Because the only thing that's going to come out of that window is your voice. And do not give him your driver's license. Simply press it up against the glass and let him read it. If you slip that license out the window and he won't give it back, I know you will get out of that car and I don't want you doing that.

The law says you have to identify yourself. That's it. You do not have to put yourself in jeopardy to make sure insurance forms are filed.

When You're Lost

If you are lost or even think you're lost, ask for help at a service station. And do it immediately. Don't wait until you have wandered into unknown, perhaps dangerous turf. That's what happened to Barbara Meller-Jensen. It happens a lot.

Men never ask for directions! But this is not something to take lightly. If it isn't a bump and run, it could be some other form of danger or violence. One family visiting relatives in Los Angeles took a wrong turn at night and found themselves in a gang-infested area of the city. Their three-year-old child was shot and killed just because they were there. That's reason enough for some of these gangbangers. Don't risk it. Ask for directions in a safe place!

Road Tips

When driving through a city, time the lights. Do not race to the next red light. If you do, you will spend more time stopped waiting for the light to change. You are more vulnerable when your vehicle is stopped. So keep it moving.

Pay attention to the people and actions happening around you, especially when stopped for a red light. That's the time most people tend to relax and ignore their surroundings. If you're talking on a cellular phone while driving you need to be especially aware . . . for your personal security and driving safety.

In parking lots, park as close to your destination as possible. If it's at night, or it will be dark before you get back to your car, park in areas that are well lit. And if you feel uncomfortable, or sense danger, get help. Ask to be escorted to your car. It doesn't matter whether your car has been parked for an hour at the mall or for a week at the airport. Believe me, they'll help you because they are told to help you by management. One of the biggest public relations nightmares for any business venture—mall, supermarket, airport, whatever—is to have someone mugged or raped on the premises.

When you leave your place of work at an odd hour, when there aren't many people around, it's the same deal. If you feel uncomfortable walking to your car, ask security to escort you.

As you drive, avoid marginal areas—places where you would not feel comfortable standing on the corner. Select routes to your destinations with this in mind. Even if you're running late for work or an appointment, don't take shortcuts through unfamiliar territory.

Here's something my mother does and it's a good idea. She keeps a baseball cap in the car and wears it whenever she is out of familiar driving territory. This gives the impression from a distance that a man is driving the car. And since women are targeted by carjackers far more often than men, this works!

Driving Defensively

Drive in the left lane whenever possible. If you have to make a maneuver, you have the whole other side of the street to work with. When you stop, leave at least half to three-quarters of a car length between your car and the one in front of you. If there's trouble, you can make your move without having to back up first.

Drive in the left lane whenever possible. If you have to make a maneuver, you have the whole other side of the street to work with.

If you are threatened and need to violate traffic regulations to ensure your safety and the safety of your passengers, sound the horn first then drive around the car or persons in front of you. Make a U-turn, go through the stop sign, or even a red light if necessary—do whatever it takes to keep from being trapped and unable to move. Then drive to where there are people and call for help. But whatever driving maneuver you make, do it safely. There is no gain if you make a turn and get hit by a bus! Safety is paramount.

Getting Gas

The FBI reported there were over 28,000 convenience store robberies in 1994. Many of these involved service stations. So you need to be especially cautious when you stop for gas. If it's at night, or you are in unfamiliar territory, go to the full-service pump. Keep the doors locked and the windows up.

If you go to a self-serve pump, turn off the engine and lock the doors when you go into the station to pay. This is especially important if you have children in the car. It takes about ten seconds for someone to snatch a child out of a car and disappear. Or if you leave the keys in the ignition, your car's gone and your kids could be in for the ride of their lives.

Hide Your Vehicle Documents

Keep the registration and insurance certificate for the vehicle in the trunk. The glove compartment and area above the sun visor are the first places searched by a thief. If he gets your registration, he's got your address. And he could be waiting for you at home, when you least expect it.

Attended Parking Lots

At an attended parking garage, leave only your ignition key. There have been many instances of parking attendants who are involved in burglary rings. Here's how it works: You give the attendant your key ring and it contains your house keys. He searches the vehicle and finds your identification. Then he calls the house to determine if anyone is home. If not, an accomplice waiting in a truck nearby makes a duplicate copy of the house key on a portable key cutter and the race is on. The guy with the key can be at your house and have it stripped clean before you get home. Since the attendant already has your phone number, he can make a quick warning call to signal your return. It's slick and almost impossible to trace. So only leave your ignition key!

Make Your Car a Tough Target

There is no way to make your vehicle 100 percent theft-proof. A professional

---

car thief can steal any car if he really wants it; make him work for yours. The best approach is common sense layered with a combination of anti-theft devices.

STEERING WHEEL LOCKS: "The Club" is the most well-known of these devices which prevent the steering wheel from being turned. They also act as a visual deterrent for thieves looking in car windows.

CAR ALARMS: The typical car alarm is equipped with motion sensors, impact sensors, and a loud siren or series of tones in the 120-decibel range. We hear car alarms going off all the time and most people ignore them, but the bad guy can't afford to ignore that noise because noise is his enemy.

The best alarms arm themselves automatically when you leave the vehicle and include an automatic kill switch. The best models also flash the headlights and honk the horn in addition to sounding a siren.

KILL SWITCHES: A kill switch is a hidden switch that needs to be flipped on for the car to start. They are, for the most part, inexpensive and easy to install. They work by preventing the flow of electricity or fuel to the engine until the switch is activated. Starter disablers are also growing in popularity.

ELECTRONIC TRACKING DEVICES: An electronic transmitter hidden in the vehicle emits a signal that is picked up by the police or monitoring station. Your assigned number and the VIN of your car are paired in a database. A routine theft report filed with the police causes a radio signal to activate the device, which then broadcasts a homing signal.

The recovery rates are extremely high with these devices and that recovery often happens before vehicles can be stripped or chopped up.

ELECTRONIC KEYS: Some car manufacturers have pre-installed electronic anti-theft systems that allow the vehicle to operate only with a correctly coded key. These are standard items in some cars and virtually invisible to thieves.

STEERING COLUMN ARMORED COLLARS: The collars prevent thieves from breaking into the steering column to hot-wire the vehicle. Some are installed permanently and others must be installed manually each time the driver leaves the vehicle.

TIRE LOCKS: These are similar to the circular steel "boots" used by many larger city police departments to nail car owners delinquent on paying outstanding tickets. They make the car virtually impossible to move and they are an excellent visual deterrent. These locks are available to the public to make thieves think the car is immobile.

VIN ETCHINGS: Etching the number onto the window—as well as other parts of the car—discourages thieves from taking the vehicle and also aids in recovering the vehicle if it is stolen.

DECALS: These identify the vehicle as being protected by either an alarm system or national theft-prevention company. The bad guys will spot a phony decal, so if you intend to try to bluff the thieves it needs to look legit.

Some guys will get your car if they really want it. Some even use tow trucks! But the idea is to make your vehicle a tougher target because the Tough Target does not get picked. That applies to you, your home, and your vehicle.

Each of the above devices can make your car more secure, but when you have more than one of these, your car becomes much safer.

Case in point: Car number one has "The Club," car number two has an alarm, car number three is in a garage, and car number four is in the garage with an alarm and "The Club." Which car is safest? Number four, of course. Each deterrent or device works with the other to make the car safer.

Carry an Emergency Kit

Remember always to have an emergency kit on hand. This should include a working flashlight and jumper cables in the car at all times. A first-aid kit and emergency blanket are other items to keep in the trunk.

I would also suggest becoming a member of a motor club. For a modest monthly or yearly fee, they offer several outstanding benefits including twenty-four-hour emergency road service, lost key/lock-out service, an arrest bond certificate, free maps and tourbooks, trip planning, discounts on hotels and car rentals, and many other benefits.

Keep in mind that most of the tips mentioned in this chapter are simple and require only minor changes in your behavior or routine. If you normally leave the keys in the car when you go to pay for gas, stop doing that. It's simple! How much time does it take to grab the keys and lock the door when you go into a service station? None at all!

Get in the habit of doing these things right and they will become second nature for you and your family. It's like wearing your safety belt. Once you get used to putting it on before starting your car, it becomes routine.

Chapter 16

TRAVELING SAFELY

For many people travel is a way of life. It may be part of their job. For others, the word evokes images of exciting experiences, different cultures and peoples, and exotic places.

Whatever the purpose, travel imposes a new set of rules on our usual routine. Unless your trip takes you into the wilderness somewhere, you shouldn't have to worry about the dangers of a marauding bear or other wild animal. But you do have to worry about human predators. There are bad guys everywhere and they're always looking for an easy target—the tourist!

When you travel—whatever your destination—you need to understand that most travelers are easy to spot and can be quickly sized up by the bad guys. They know you are probably carrying more cash than usual, there may be expensive jewelry in your luggage, and you're not on your own turf. But they are! That tips the scales heavily in their favor. So how do you keep paradise from becoming a jungle? Let's start with your plan.

Planning for Safety

It all begins with a solid plan. You need to research your destination. Know ahead of time what you are going to do, where you are going to go, and how you are going to get there safely. There are plenty of resources to check out—magazines, books, travel guides, and travel agents—to help with your planning. This is especially important if your travel takes you to an international or unusual destination where you may not understand all the customs.

An important part of that planning begins with your home. When you leave for any extended period of time, your home is more vulnerable than ever. The burglars may have been watching your house and are aware of your routine.

More burglaries occur in July and August than in other months and vacationing families are a large factor. Certainly nobody wants to return from a nice trip to find their home burglarized. So let's start there.

Before Leaving Home

First, you want your home to be occupied or appear to be occupied. Consider having a friend stay over, or employ a bonded house-sitting service. If neither of those options works for you, arrange to have someone—a friend or trusted neighbor—go to your home every day to pick up the mail and check on any other deliveries. Make sure that person knows how to reach you in case of emergency.

- Cancel your newspaper delivery. If there are newspapers lying at the front door, you might as well put an Open House sign out front because your home is an instant target.
- Pay someone to shovel your driveway or mow the grass.
- Be sure blinds and curtains are closed. Check automatic timers to be sure both exterior and interior lights come on at night.

Inside, it's a good idea to have lights come on automatically in at least two rooms. It's also a good idea to put a timer on a radio, so there's noise inside, especially in the evening hours. Arm your home security system and be sure the monitoring company knows you are out of town and has a number where to reach you.

Be sure doors and windows are locked, including the garage door. If you have a phone-answering machine, do not indicate in any way on your message that you are out of town. And pick up messages periodically while you are away.

And finally, notify the police of your travel plans. Most departments will alert patrol cars to keep an eye on your home.

Make a Backup Itinerary

Leave your itinerary with a friend or trusted neighbor. Make three copies of your important documents, such as credit cards, passport, visa, traveler's check numbers, and driver's license. Keep a copy in your luggage (this could be a special compartment in a carry-on bag), a copy in your office, and one in your home or the home of a relative. Wherever you go and whatever you lose, someone will be able to fax your identification to you. They will also have a list of the credit cards and their numbers so the cards can be canceled if lost or stolen. Leave that information behind along with your itinerary. If everything is lost or stolen, you have recourse.

Use Traveler's Checks

Do not carry large amounts of cash. Cash is a thief's dream. Use traveler's checks instead. Sign the checks as instructed, record the numbers, and keep that information separate from the checks. If they are lost or stolen, notify the traveler's check company immediately. So be sure to have their phone number with you when you travel. And never countersign a check until you are ready to cash it.

Traveling by Car

If you are traveling by car, take your vehicle in for a complete maintenance checkup before you leave. That provides peace of mind for you and your family and it can keep you out of trouble. You are vulnerable in a broken-down vehicle on the side of the road. And remember, doors locked and windows up at all times! Be sure to teach your children this.

Along with the maps, car registration, and other travel-related information you bring, include your cellular phone, pepper spray, a working flashlight, and a first-aid kit. Make it all part of one safety pack and it won't be a big deal.

Travel lightly. Most people take way too much stuff. Go for function first and style second. The less luggage you take, the less chance there is for loss or theft. Put your name and business address—not your home address—on luggage ID tags.

Rental Car Review

These days, many rental car companies have implemented a number of safety-related changes. The telltale Y or Z on rental license plates that marked that car as a rental vehicle has been removed, along with promotional stickers, logos, and other labels that identify a car as a rental vehicle.

Most rental car outlets in larger cities can also provide portable cellular phones. It's a quick link to the police if you get in trouble. For about five dollars a day, it might just save your life! That's a good investment in my book. In some cities and with some companies, you can request a car equipped with high-tech equipment that includes an electronic mapping system and a panic button to signal police.

Some of the larger companies offer computerized step-by-step directions at most major airports to provide the most direct and safest route to your destination.

Be aware of your options when renting a car and make sure, at the very least, that the car you rent is unmarked. And don't mark yourself either. There is nothing that says "tourist" more loudly than a man driving a freshly washed car with a woman in the passenger seat reading a map and the backseat piled high with luggage.

Traveling by Airplane

If you are traveling by airplane, have tickets sent to you in advance with boarding passes included. Get to the airport early, check bags immediately, and move through security to the gate. Do not leave any carry-on luggage unattended—even for a moment.

Why is there such a high concentration of police at the airports? To offset a high concentration of bad guys! Don't be deceived by appearances. If some guy is hanging around a gate area looking to steal a bag, he's not going to look and act like a street bum. That would put everyone on alert. Chances are he'll look like any other traveler.

One of the newest targets for theft is the laptop computer. These machines routinely sell for as much as $5,000 and are easy to fence or resell. Here is how it works: As the unsuspecting businessman is approaching the X-ray machine at the security checkpoint at the airport, he draws the attention of the two thieves. Thief number one passes through the metal detector and waits on the secure side. The other thief gets in front of the target with the laptop computer.

As the victim is putting his computer on the conveyor belt, the second bad guy gets in front of the victim and walks through the metal detector. The machine beeps and he steps back. He removes the keys from his pocket and tries again. Meanwhile the computer has passed through the conveyor belt and is waiting on the other side. The businessman is still being stalled by number two, who still cannot seem to pass through the detector without setting it off.

Bad guy number one picks up the computer and walks away. Probably right back out the exit door, past the two men, and into a car. This whole thing takes less than twenty seconds. It can happen to a purse as well. And don't let anybody fool you. The thieves know that the money and jewelry are in the purse not in the luggage.

Safety at Hotels and Motels

When you arrive at the hotel, take the time to locate fire exits. Your best choice for a room is on floors two through seven. You're off the ground level on the second floor, and still within easy reach of a ladder, in case of fire. If the ground floor is your only choice for a room, be sure to lock your windows and the sliding-glass door. If there is no bar to secure the sliding-glass door, call the desk and ask for one. Sliding-glass doors can be easy targets for illegal entry to a hotel room, just as they are in the home.

Let the bellman take you to your room, open the door, and turn on the lights. If you are not escorted to your room, do as the flight attendants do. They open the door and prop it open with a piece of luggage, turn on the lights, and check out the room. They look in the closets, under the bed, and in the bathroom. If someone is hiding out, that door is open for a quick escape. Then they close and double-lock the door.

Most hotels have the television tuned to the hotel channel. When you turn the TV on, the hotel safety video will play. This is a hotel-specific video explaining the safety policies and security procedures of the hotel. Watch the video and have the kids watch it too.

What happens to a hotel hit with a rash of crimes? It's simple. Customers go elsewhere. But only if those crimes become public knowledge. So it's tempting to deal with the problem in-house rather than reporting crimes to the police.

A few years ago, at a first-class Portland, Oregon, hotel, the security director came running when he heard loud blasts from a gun. Through a crack in the door, he saw someone standing over a bloodied body, reloading a shotgun, apparently ready to go on a rampage through the hotel.

The security director put his life on the line to subdue and arrest this guy. But his heroics didn't get much attention within the hotel chain itself, or with local media. The whole affair was kept as quiet as possible.

Of course, no hotel wants a murder to become a media event. But sweeping crimes under the rug is not an answer either. That's a problem the industry is working hard to minimize but it's one you need to be aware of.

You may not know what the track record is of a hotel or motel when it comes to crime, but you can select a property with good security.

Assessing Hotel Security

You should have a list of questions to ask when making hotel or motel reservations: cost, amenities, restaurants, health club, proximity to tourist attractions and business destinations. After reading this, I know you'll make a habit of putting security on the top of your list.

Ask the following questions:

- What is the specific location? Is it in a safe part of town? (That alone can keep you out of trouble.)
- Does the facility have key cards or metal keys? You want the key card!
- Is there round-the-clock security? Are there surveillance cameras on the floors? Is there controlled access to elevators and parking facilities?

These questions indicate to the hotel that you take security seriously. The answers will indicate to you whether they do.

Find the Fire Exits

Check out the fire exits and review the instructions in case of fire. That information is posted on the back of the door. Because you never use elevators in a fire, count the number of doors between your room and the fire exit door. Even though the exit sign is illuminated, dense smoke may prevent you from seeing it.

There is a lot more to know about surviving a fire and this is not intended to be a primer on that topic. But there are thousands of hotel fires every year in which lives are lost. So a few common sense precautions might save your life.

Use the Hotel Safe

You are carrying traveler's checks instead of large amounts of cash, so that's good. But do not leave the checks or any other valuables—airline tickets, passports, keys, credit cards, cameras, jewelry—in your room. Those items belong in the hotel safe or on your person. At most hotels, the safe is a free service. Take advantage of it.

PHILIP MARTIN AND JACK THOMPSON

Philip Martin and Jack Thompson found that out the hard way. Phil and Jack were experienced business travelers but they checked into a hotel that was lax in security. That nearly spelled disaster.

After a series of successful business meetings, Phil and Jack took a cab to their hotel and checked in. At the counter, they were greeted by a courteous desk clerk who took their credit cards and pulled their registration forms. While they waited, Phil and Jack talked openly about the big deal they had just closed. They were ready to relax and celebrate their victory.

Phil's briefcase held the spoils of their deal, thousands of dollars in negotiable bearer bonds. Jack told Phil to put the briefcase in the hotel safe. But Phil told Jack he was being paranoid and an argument followed. Jack finally agreed that he was being overly cautious so they brought the briefcase into the room. They were not being particularly loud or boisterous—but they were loud enough.

Sitting within earshot was a handsome couple, well dressed and fashionable. They blended perfectly with the plush surroundings of the lobby. No one would have guessed their purpose in being there. Here's how it came down:

CLERK: Gentlemen, your keys. Mr. Martin, you're in room 1120. Mr. Thompson, you're just down the hall in 1134.

> *PHIL AND JACK SIGNED THEIR REGISTRATION FORMS, GRABBED THEIR BAGS, AND HEADED FOR THE ELEVATORS. THEY HAD NO IDEA THEY HAD BEEN MARKED. A SHORT TIME LATER THEY MET IN PHIL'S ROOM, OPENED A BOTTLE OF SCOTCH, AND BEGAN THEIR CELEBRATION.*

PHIL: To a successful trip!

JACK: To a successful deal! Cheers!

> *THEN THEY REMINISCED AND JOKED. A FEW MINUTES LATER, THERE WAS A KNOCK ON THE DOOR.*

WOMAN: Housekeeping.

PHIL: Just a minute.

> *PHIL OPENED THE DOOR A CRACK WITHOUT GIVING IT A SECOND THOUGHT.*

PHIL: We didn't call . . .

> *BAM! THE DOOR FLEW OPEN AND SOMEONE KNOCKED PHIL DOWN WITH A VICIOUS BACKHAND TO THE HEAD. THERE WAS A PISTOL IN HIS HAND AND THE WELL-DRESSED COUPLE FROM THE LOBBY WAS IN THE ROOM.*

WOMAN: Be quiet and nobody'll get hurt. Toss your wallets on the bed. And the watches too. Move!

JACK: Now just a minute here . . .

THE MAN WITH THE GUN STEPPED CLOSER AND WAVED THE PISTOL AT THE TWO MEN.

THEY REALIZED HE MEANT BUSINESS AND JACK BACKED OFF.

MAN: You heard the lady. Shut up and do as she says.

PHIL AND JACK TOSSED THEIR WALLETS AND WATCHES ONTO THE BED.

WOMAN: And don't worry about the briefcase—I'll take it off your hands.

JACK: How did you know . . . ?

WOMAN: It's simple. You and your buddy here got big mouths, hotshot.

THE WOMAN GRABBED THE BRIEFCASE FROM THE TABLE AND HANDED IT TO HER

ACCOMPLICE. SHE GATHERED THE WALLETS AND WATCHES FROM THE BED.

WOMAN: Gentlemen, it's been a pleasure doing business with you.

MAN: Now you boys sit real quiet because I'm going to be standing right outside this door for the next two minutes. If you pick up that phone it'll be the last thing you'll ever do. You got that?

IN A FLASH THEY WERE GONE. PHIL AND JACK DID AS THEY WERE TOLD.

What happened to Phil and Jack is not an isolated incident. And despite losing a small fortune in negotiable bonds—which can be easily converted to cash—it could have been worse. They could have lost their lives. And the bad guys in this incident? They worked as a team. They were also smart and shrewd, which sets them apart from most common street criminals. They didn't look like the bad guy at the bus stop or a creep hanging around the mall. But they can be intimidating and very dangerous.

Phil and Jack, like most guests in hotels and motels, assumed their safety was assured by the hotel. They let down their guard and you can't do that. Even in hotels with good security, that's not something you want to do. Especially in hotels or motels with poor security—these places are prime hunting grounds for criminals.

Leaving Your Room

When you leave your room, turn on a light and the radio or television set. That gives the appearance the room is occupied and that alone makes it a tougher target. The burglars are looking for unoccupied rooms.

When I leave a hotel room to go out, I walk out the door and before I close it, I talk back into the empty room and say, "I'll be back in twenty minutes." It takes no time at all and gives the impression that there is someone in the room and that I will be back soon.

When you return to your room in the evening, use the main entrance. If you see someone lurking around the entrance or in the halls, report it to the front desk. Once in your room, use the bolt and chain. Your personal alarm can also double as a door or window alarm if it includes a special adapter. Simply replace the pull cord with the accessory cord and insert the contact clip between the door or window and its frame. If the door or window is opened, the alarm goes off, and because the bad guys are afraid of noise, you'll be okay.

Verifying Visitors

If someone knocks on your door, use the peephole to check out who is there. If the person claims to be a hotel employee and you're unsure, call the front desk to verify that they're legitimate. As Phil and Jack discovered, things are not always as they seem. Don't be fooled by uniforms. Uniforms can be easily rented or stolen.

Robbery

If you do find yourself face-to-face with a bad guy who's in your room, it's no different from any other robbery situation. Give up the property and get him out of there as quickly as possible. Most of the time, the bad guys want that property and do not want confrontation. But if you are faced with rape or other violent acts, do what you need to do to survive.

Traveling Abroad

If you live in Memphis and travel to Phoenix, you are not on your home turf but at least it's familiar turf. You speak the language and you know the laws. Often in other countries, you are playing on unfamiliar turf—different customs, a foreign language, and strange currency. So you need to take special precautions when traveling out of the country.

First, check with the U.S. Department of State. They offer an Overseas Citizen Services helpline that provides information on political and social conditions in your destination country. Call: (202) 647-5225.

Notify the U.S. Embassy of your itinerary. Know how to contact police and doctors in the native language. Learn how to use pay telephones with the correct change on hand in case of emergency. Choose hotels using the same criteria you do at home, by making security a priority issue. When you leave the hotel, have the hotel arrange for reliable local transportation.

When you travel between countries, be courteous with customs officers. Have passports and other documents available. Answer questions directly and honestly. Keep a low profile and try to blend in with the citizenry. Dress conservatively. Avoid jewelry that identifies with a certain religion. When using an ATM card in a foreign country, use the same precautions as you would at home. If you are on a group tour, stay with the group. Be cautious when choosing sightseeing trips. Check with the hotel concierge about tours or side trips. The adventure of a lifetime touted by a local hustler may turn out to be more than you bargained for! Or it might be your last adventure.

Reviewing Resorts

From the exotic to the sublime, resorts are enjoying growing popularity as vacation destinations. Partly because of this popularity, and partly due to the casual nature of most of these places, resorts tend to be magnets for all kinds of bad guys: burglars, armed robbers, con artists, pimps, prostitutes, and pickpockets. Whatever type—you name them and they're there.

LISA SHIRLEY

Lisa Shirley, a flight attendant living in a Dallas suburb, can certainly attest to that. On a vacation trip to Antigua with her husband and some friends, Lisa faced the worst kind of predator. This is the letter she wrote to me:

"My husband, friends, and I were sitting at an outdoor horseshoe-shaped bar about 100 yards from the beach with a loud band playing. I went to the bathroom, which was very close but out of sight of those at the bar.

"As I approached the bathroom, I suddenly felt arms go around me in a bear hug from behind. A man started dragging me backwards. I yelled and managed to break free, only to be caught again. This time the man spun me around and put me in a choke hold and held a gun to my head with his other hand.

"He began dragging me away from the bar toward a dirt path. I could see his accomplice about twenty feet ahead, watching as we moved toward him. I remembered the small purse hanging from my shoulder and offered it to him. He replied, 'I don't want your purse, you're coming with me.' I knew I was in big trouble! I knew that if I went with him, I'd be hurt or killed. I decided to take my chances trying to get away.

I grabbed the gun with my right hand and pulled it away from my head while using my left hand to free myself from his choke hold. The next thing I knew, I had flipped him to the ground. I started to run but he was determined and grabbed my calves, pulling me to the ground. His gun had scooted across the ground when he fell and was now within my reach.

"I knew he was not going to let go of me and so I grabbed the gun—a .45 caliber, I found out later—with the intent to shoot him. Before I could aim the gun at him, he grabbed for it and we struggled for a while so I let go of the gun, got to my feet, and ran. I never looked back.

"The police never caught this guy or his accomplice, although when they examined the crime scene they found a .45 caliber bullet, his broken watch which I had torn from his wrist, my shoes, and even my missing earring. I feel so fortunate to have been able to walk away with only a split elbow.

"Before we had gone on that trip, my husband and I had been watching your *Street Smarts* on PBS. In that show, you talked about how you should never get into a car or go anywhere with someone who is trying to take you to the secondary crime scene.

"Before seeing that show, I had never thought about what I would do in a situation. I have never had any self-defense training, but that night I decided I would put up a fight and try to escape if anything like that ever happened to me. You think it won't happen to you, but it can! That show saved my life!"

This incident didn't happen to Lisa at two o'clock in the morning in a dark alley. She was attacked in broad daylight. So remember, you can't let your guard down anytime.

I'm proud of Lisa and what she did. She had a plan and she refused to be taken to the secondary crime scene.

Wherever you are, and whenever you travel, that advice can save your life.

Tips for Terrorism

Despite the bombings of the World Trade Center and the federal building in Oklahoma City, terrorism usually involves airplane travel.

The odds of being involved in a crime of terrorism are extremely remote. But if it does happen to you, there are things you can do to minimize your risk.

The most important thing—and this applies to travel in general—is to blend in. Avoid extremes in clothes and behavior. Select a window seat. Do not carry any identification like the following: company affiliation, especially if you are an executive; employment with the government; or military status—active, retired, reserve.

Keep in mind that to the terrorist, the bargaining chip is you and your fellow hostages. It's in the best interests of the terrorists to keep you alive. And keep in mind that the overwhelming number of hostage situations are resolved by negotiation and end in eventual release. To improve the odds of that happening, evaluate the motivations of the hostage taker.

Listen but do not necessarily agree with the terrorists—agreeing can be interpreted as being either weak or condescending. Do not be overly aggressive and do not be overly compliant. Do not resist their demands and give only the information that is asked for. This is no time to think you're a hero by being arrogant or abrasive. That can get you and others hurt or even killed. It might work for James Bond but it won't for you.

Stay calm and be observant. Hostages will be debriefed afterwards. Think constantly about your options: what you will do and how you will react. Avoid talking to other passengers, especially in whispers. Terrorists can be ruthless but they are often nervous, and whispering will only make them more nervous.

Prepare yourself mentally for what could be a long ordeal because the authorities view time as an important ally. Remember, the primary objective of law enforcement worldwide is the preservation of human life. And time allows them to greatly improve the odds of accomplishing their objective by wearing down the hostage taker, gathering information, negotiating, and, as a last resort, preparing for an assault.

If a rescue attempt is made, chances are there will be chaos and shooting. There are no rules here except to dive for cover, stay out of the crossfire, and follow the instructions of the counter terrorist team. I've worked with such a team before. They are quick and they are good at what they do. Let them do their job.

Finally, seek psychological help following such an ordeal. These situations are very traumatic and it's a good idea to talk about, rather than repress, your feelings. Hopefully you'll never have to deal with such a situation, but it's always better to be prepared and have a plan.

Tough Target Strategies

- Tough Target is an attitude
- The predators don't want a challenge, they want to score. The lion never goes after the strongest or the swiftest antelope. Neither does the bad guy.
- Remember the faulty logic equation: The victim says, "It won't happen to me." And the bad guy says, "I won't get caught."
- There are no absolutes. Nothing works every time.
- Remember the four laws of the jungle:
  Crime can happen to anyone, anytime, anywhere.
  The bad guys don't all look like Charles Manson, Freddie Krueger, or Bluto.
  It's not how tough you are. It's how tough he thinks you are.
- You are responsible for yourself. You need to be prepared.
- Remember the words common to virtually every victim of random crime: "It happened so fast!"

BOOK I
HAVING A PLAN
- Acknowledge your need to have a plan. Commit yourself to it.
- Keep your plan simple. Know what you are going to do before the crime happens.
- Look tough! Always walk and carry yourself in a confident manner. The Tough Target does not get selected.
- Be aware of what's going on around you at all times.
- Trust your instincts. That gut feeling is telling you, "There's trouble here."
- The bad guys will always lie. Don't forget that!
- If confronted, give up the property: purse, coat, wallet, car. Nothing you own is worth risking your life over.
- Get your knees in the breeze. If fleeing is an option, it is always your best option.
- Whatever you're going to do, do it right away.

DENYING PRIVACY
- The secondary crime scene is the deadliest piece of ground in the world. Don't ever forget that.
- If he wants more than property? If he wants you? Don't get in the car—it's a one-way trip.
- Invest in a cellular phone, especially for your car.
- If you're confronted, give up the property and get out of there. Remember, there is nothing you own that is worth risking your life over.
- What if he has a gun? Remember the 50/25/12½ progression! Weigh it out. The odds are in your favor.
- Whatever you're going to do, do it right away. The time of the initial confrontation is the time when the offender has the least amount of control over the situation.
- Cabs: Check the driver's picture ID. Comment on the registration number.
- Trains & Buses: Sit next to the driver or conductor.

ATTRACTING ATTENTION
- Yell FIRE! FIRE! FIRE! not HELP! Fire gets everyone's attention.
- If you see or hear someone else in trouble, take action.
- Use your cellular phone to call for help. Even if you don't have a cellular phone, say you do. The bad guy won't know and he can't risk it.
- If you are attacked and get knocked down, swivel around on your backside and kick for all you're worth.
- Go for the groin, shins, eyes, or throat. These are his most vulnerable areas.

TAKING ACTION
- Carry a money clip with your "get out of trouble" money.
- Keep housekeys in your pocket, not in your handbag.
- Be aware at the bank. Get a stack of withdrawal slips and keep them in your bag until you are ready to hand them over to the teller.
- Don't frequent ATMs alone at night.

EXERCISING IN SAFETY
- Wear a fanny pack with pepper spray and a personal alarm.
- Avoid headsets.
- Don't wear provocative exercise gear on the street.
- Exercise with a friend—human or canine.

- Avoid exercising in isolated areas.
- Early morning is the best time to exercise.

AVOIDING SECLUDED PLACES

- If you drop someone off at home, wait until that person is safely inside before leaving.
- Create a commotion if you think someone else is in trouble.
- Stairwells: Stay out of stairwells unless it is an emergency.
- Elevators: Avoid being alone on an elevator with someone you're uncomfortable with. If you do get confronted, push all the buttons and be prepared to fight your attacker to do it.

BOOK II

PROTECTING YOUR CHILDREN

- "Don't talk to strangers" is not enough. Role-playing works. Even better is to have a friend or colleague the child does not know approach the child. See how the child responds, and take your cue from that.
- If approached by a stranger, instruct your children to say No! Run, and yell Stranger. Stranger. Stranger.
- If the child is approached by someone in a car, run in the opposite direction the car is pointing. Before the child runs, tell the child to DROP THE BOOKS!
- When it comes to any type of forced affection, empower your children to say no to an adult.
- Teach them to travel a specified and safe route to school. No shortcuts.
- Have the child walk with a friend.
- Get to know their friends.
- If the stranger has a gun, the child must ignore the gun, ignore the threat, and run!
- Give the child simple instructions on where to run.
- Arm the child with a personal alarm that has an identifying label on it.
- Use a password for emergency situations. Pick two words that don't go together.
- Build a communication with your kids.
- Teach your children the three easy steps if they find a handgun in your home or somebody else's home: Stop—Don't Touch—Tell an Adult.
- Children left home alone must never acknowledge they are alone. They should screen calls on an answering machine, never open the door to a stranger, and know how to contact the police in an emergency.

STAYING SAFE ON CAMPUS

- Make the issue of safety and security one that is part of your evaluation process in choosing a college or university.
- Recognize that most crimes committed on college campuses—about 80 percent—are committed by other students. So keep doors locked and valuables at home.
- Be sure your daughter takes special note of the chapter on rape. She needs to know that if an acquaintance or date becomes aggressive, he needs to be treated as if he were a total stranger. No means NO!
- Use the checklist in this chapter as a reference.
- Don't be afraid to ask hard questions.
- Request a copy of the federal crime report from the admissions office.
- Request a report on off-campus crimes, especially if your son or daughter intends to live off campus.
- Remember that alcohol is a contributing factor in a large majority of rapes and sexual assaults.
- If your son or daughter chooses to drink, encourage them to do so responsibly.
- Check out what measures are being taken by the school to encourage such behavior and to discourage alcohol abuse.

SAFETY-CONSCIOUS SENIORS

- When you go out, attach a chain to your glasses, wear a fanny pack, carry a pepper spray or alarm.
- If confronted, give up property immediately and move away from the scene as quickly as you are able. Don't plead or bargain or beg.
- Use your voice.
- Keep your money and other valuables in the bank. Use direct deposit for government checks.
- Participate in a neighborhood watch program and establish daily contact with family or neighbors.
- Lock your doors when working outside around the home.
- If you are victimized . . . report it!
- Be wary of the con artist. Remember, they are aggressive, persuasive, and smart.
- If an offer seems too good to be true—it is!
- Do a thorough background check on anyone you are considering for home repairs.
- Never give private information over the phone—like credit card or phone card numbers. The number one tip-off to fraud is a high-pressure approach.

Spotting the Wolf in Sheep's Clothing
- Stalking. Learn to recognize the three classic warning signs:
  When you say no he gets enraged.
  He will exhibit wild mood swings and start snooping into your private life.
  He will turn up uninvited at work, at home, or while you are out with friends.
- Contact the police immediately at the first incident; report all subsequent violations of the law.
  Get a copy of the stalking law in your state.
- Make your rejection final! Do not negotiate.
- Alter your routine: what, where, and when you do things. Change your phone number to one that is unlisted.
- Document everything. Save letters, phone messages, keep a personal diary, confide in a friend . . . all evidence that may be needed for a restraining order.
- Work with authorities to get a conviction.
- Serial killers: Be aware. Be smart. Trust no stranger and never go anywhere with someone you don't know.
- The Casanova: Learn to recognize the warning signs of the Casanova. He'll zero in on your financial affairs very quickly.

Responding to Rape
- No woman asks or deserves to be raped. No matter what the circumstances may be.
- Your body language, your look, your tone of voice, and your verbal response are all crucial in dealing with aggressive behavior.
- If you can flee, flee. If you can't, and you decide to fight, go in 100 percent committed!
- If an acquaintance or date becomes aggressive, treat him as if he was a total stranger. No matter who it is, no means NO!
- Firmly and directly say, "You are out of line and I'm not interested. Now leave me alone."
- Bite down on his lower lip as he tries to kiss you.
- A provocative manner and provocative clothing can solicit unwanted attention.
- Be responsible with the consumption of alcohol and be aware of its influence on yourself and others.
- If you are raped, tell your parents or a trusted friend at once. And call the police immediately.
- Don't change clothes or bathe after a rape.
- Get professional help from a counselor or therapist. Find a support group for rape victims and talk about your experience as soon as you can.
- Don't blame yourself. It's not your fault.

Violence in the Workplace
- You have a right to a safe and secure workplace environment. But you must do your part: Speak up, ask questions, get involved.
- Remember that you are responsible for your own safety. Don't be overly reliant on anyone else, including your employer.
- Abide by the rules of the organization. This means following procedures and adhering to guidelines for hiring and firing personnel.
- Be aware. You are the eyes and ears of the company. It means getting management involved, especially if you believe a fellow employee is exhibiting unusual behavior patterns.
- Be aware of the typical warning signs that often precede violent behavior. These include: inconsistent work patterns and decreased efficiency, evidence of unusual stress, unpredictable mood swings, exaggerated personality traits.
- Be aware of the four primary ways in which workplace violence manifests itself:
  Through robbery or theft.
  Spillover from domestic abuse.
  Violence directed at an employer.
  An act of terrorism or hate.

Choosing Your Weapon
- Remember, guns, knives, hat pins, keys, stun guns, whistles are not your best options for personal protection.
- Invest in a good pepper spray and personal alarm and learn how to use them.
- Consider a self-defense course that teaches personal empowerment as the foundation of the program.

BOOK III
Securing Your Home
- The best deterrent to home burglaries and robberies is a monitored home security system.
- Get a dog!

- Buy a big dog bowl and write Killer on it and put it outside your door.
- Where you choose to live is one of the most important factors influencing risks of all types of crime. So choose your location wisely if you are moving or plan a move.
- Be sure your home looks tough. Keep hedges trimmed, curtains closed, and lights on at night when you're away.
- Good exterior and interior lighting are both important. Consider motion-control lighting for the exterior and timers for the interior.
- Consult with a professional for your locks.
- Secure sliding glass doors with a safety bar that has an anti-lift feature.
- Doors should be made of steel with a steel frame, or metal wrapped over solid-core wood.
- Keep doors and windows locked, especially when you are home. This includes the garage door!
- Create a safe room within your home.
- Get involved. Participate in a neighborhood watch program.

SAFEGUARDING YOUR CAR

- If you leave the vehicle, no matter how short the time, don't leave it unlocked or the keys in the ignition for any reason.
- In a parking lot, approach your car with keys and pepper spray in hand. Be aware of your surroundings. Look around, under, and in your car before getting in. If you sense danger, go back to the store and ask for an escort.
- Packages and a child: When you get to the car, first put the packages in the trunk. Next, put the child in the car seat. Then get in the car, lock the doors, and start the engine. Finally, reach over and strap the child in the seat.
- If someone approaches with a weapon and he gets to you before the door is locked—give him the car.
- Keep a set of trick keys hidden on the steering wheel column. If he wants the car and you, toss those trick keys as far as you can throw them, preferably under another car. When he goes for the keys, get out of there.
- To avoid the smash and grab, keep your purse or other valuables on the floor, not on the seat.
- When you drive, wear your safety belt and keep the doors locked and the windows up at all times.
- Women should wear a baseball hat when driving alone at night.
- If you break down on the highway, or someone motions you over, or you get bumped, do not get out of the car. Use your cellular phone to call for help. Put a HELP! CALL POLICE! sign in the window and ask someone else to call for you.
- Do not relinquish your driver's license and never accept a ride from a stranger.
- Be smart about where, when, how you drive—don't take shortcuts into unfamiliar territory.
- Give only your ignition key to a parking attendant.
- Consider a car alarm or other security device.
- Become a member of a motor club.

TRAVELING SAFELY

- Safeguard your home. It should look occupied. Have a neighbor or friend pick up mail and mow the lawn or shovel the driveway. Cancel the newspaper.
- Be sure all doors and windows are locked, including the garage. Arm your home security system and notify the monitoring company on how to reach you.
- Notify the police you will be out of town.
- Bring a safety pack that includes a cellular phone, pepper spray, first-aid kit, and flashlight.
- Use a professional travel agency. Carry traveler's checks, not large amounts of cash.
- If traveling by plane, get to the airport early, check luggage, and move through security to the gate area right away. Do not leave carry-on bags unattended.
- Have the bellman escort you to your room; check out the fire exits; leave a light and the TV on when leaving the room; use all locks when in the room; never let anyone you don't know inside without verifying who it is.
- Have the hotel arrange for ground transportation.
- For international travel, check out your intended destination in advance; keep a low profile; dress conservatively; know how to contact the police or a doctor in the native language. Keep the correct amount of change on hand in case of emergency. Notify the U.S. Embassy of your itinerary.
- Terrorism: The chances of being involved in a crime of terrorism are remote.
- Do not be overly aggressive and do not be overly compliant with the terrorists.
- If a rescue attempt is made, lay low and follow the instructions of the counter terrorist team.

ABOUT THE AUTHOR

J.J. Bittenbinder is America's leading expert on crime and personal safety. A twenty-three year veteran of the Chicago Police Department, where he served as a detective in homicide and violent crimes, he is a recognized authority on assault prevention and crime-scene investigation, training and instruction. During his career, Bittenbinder has interviewed more than 1,000 witnesses, victims, and offenders involved in violent street crime. Combining a dynamic presence with a powerful message, Bittenbinder is known throughout the country from his *Tough Target* television series, his regular appearances on *Good Morning America,* and PBS's *Street Smarts.* He is currently an inspector with the Cook County Sheriff's Department and travels widely bringing his safety strategies to schools, community organizations, and corporate groups.